CONTENTS

Introduction 5
Breakfast 6
- Broccoli Parmesan Casserole 6
- Chicken Sausages 6
- Oats Carrot Cookies 7
- Avocado Cheddar Rolls 7
- Turmeric Potato Pancakes 8
- Cheddar Eggs Burrito 8
- Scrambled Eggs 9
- Turkey Bread Reuben 9
- English Eggs Bacon Breakfast 10
- Turmeric Potato 10
- Milky Vanilla Toasts 11
- Creamy Bacon Omelet 11
- Baked Cheddar Eggs 12
- Bacon Zucchini Boats 12
- Breakfast Parmesan Sandwich 13
- Cheddar Baked Paprika Toasts 13
- Egg Ham Rolls 14
- Buttery Potato Scramble 14
- Sugary Oatmeal Muffins 15
- Tofu Potato Scramble 15
- Cinnamon French Toast 16
- Vanilla Bread Pudding 17
- Mozzarella Sausage Stromboli 17
- Strawberry Oatmeal 18
- Cheddar Hash Browns 18
- Cheddar Bread Pizza 19
- Mozzarella Pepperoni Patties 19
- Paprika Soufflé 20
- Tabasco Chicken Meatballs 20
- Cheddar Zucchini Frittata 21
- Milky Cod 21
- Chicken Mushroom Rolls 22
- Running Cheddar Eggs 22
- Cheddar Potato Halves 23
- Chicken Strips 24
- Wrapped Bacon Eggs 24
- Banana Pancakes 25
- Honey Pumpkin Mash 25
- Cheese Oatmeal Fritters 26
- Parmesan Spinach Quiche 26
- Egg Sandwich 27
- Eggs in Bacon Cups 27
- Leek Parmesan Tarts 28
- Avocado Eggs 28
- Smoked Salmon Omelet 29
- Paprika Chicken Buns 29
- Parmesan Chorizo Rolls 30
- Cheddar Crumpets 30

Main Dishes 31
- Pork Strips 31
- Pineapple Chicken Breast 31
- Catfish Nuggets 32
- Creamy Coriander Tilapia 32
- Italian Beer Cod 33
- Garlic Catfish 33
- Turmeric Snapper 34
- Orange Beef Mignon 34
- Chicken Oatmeal Schnitzel 35
- Salty Pork Belly 35
- Ribeye Beef Steak 36
- Garlic Ground Chicken 36
- Pork Chops 37
- Crunchy Catfish 37
- Celery Chicken Wings 38
- Rosemary Beef Steak 38
- Creamy Cod Fillet 39
- Butter Chicken Drumsticks 39
- Thyme Lamb Ribs 40
- Curry Chicken Breast 40
- Maple Turkey Breast 41
- Rosemary Salmon Steak 41
- Stuffed Calamari 42
- Paprika Corn Beef 42
- Dijon Turkey Legs 43
- Beef Zucchini Rings 43
- Parmesan Peppers 44
- Cabbage Beef Rolls 45
- Pork Bak 46
- Chili Pork Slices 47
- Onion Chicken Skin 48
- Oregano Pork Loaf 48
- Tender Beef Burgers 49
- Honey Pork Meatballs 49
- Cheddar Chicken Breast 50
- Garlic Pork Satay 50
- Ginger Paprika Shrimps 51
- Tomato Beef 51
- Cayenne Lamb Steak 52
- Rosemary Lamb Shank 53
- Turmeric Chicken Necks 53
- Yogurt Chicken Kebab 54
- Dijon Chicken 54
- Pork Ribs 55
- Coconut Chili Beef Strips 55
- Oat Chicken Sausages 56

Side Dishes 57
- Parmesan Sweet Potato Casserole 57
- Spicy Zucchini Slices 57
- Cheddar Potato Gratin 58
- Salty Lemon Artichokes 58
- Asparagus & Parmesan 59
- Carrot Lentil Burgers 59
- Corn on Cobs 60
- Sugary Carrot Strips 60
- Onion Green Beans 61
- Mozzarella Radish Salad 61
- Cremini Mushroom Satay 62
- Eggplant Ratatouille 62
- Cheddar Portobello Mushrooms 63
- Creamy Cauliflower Head 63
- Cream Cheese Baked Potato 64
- Cayenne Pepper Brussels Sprouts 64
- Bell Pepper Slices 65
- Sugary Pumpkin Wedges 65

Cream Cheese Spinach 66
Creamy Leek 66
Paprika Hasselback Potatoes 67
Marinated Eggplants with Sesame Seeds 67
Cheddar Mac'n'Cheese 68
White Oregano Cabbage 68
Creamy Broccoli Florets 69
Dill Mashed Potato 69
Butternut Squash Puree 70
Cream Potato 70
Tomato Nutmeg Zucchini 71
Cabbage with Tomato 72
Oregano Garlic Heads 73
Feta Beet Cubes 73
Eggplant & Zucchini Mix 74
Chard with Cheddar 75
Sweet Potato Cubes 75
Sweet Onion Rings 76
Olive Oil Okra 76
Mushrooms & Cream 77
Mexican Parmesan Corn 77
Tahini Eggplants 78
Cream Cheese Cauliflower 78
Feta Cheese Potato Slices 79
Thyme Fennel 79
Chili Squash Wedges 80
Paprika Yellow Squash 80
Puff Cauliflower Patties 81
Cottage Cheese Mushrooms 81
Honey Carrots with Greens 82
Creamy Red Potatoes 82
Snacks and Appetizers 83
Sesame Tofu Cubes 83
Thyme Salty Tomatoes 83
Creamy Chicken Liver 84
Catfish Sticks 84
Honey Banana Chips 85
Ginger Apple Chips 85
Maple Carrot Fries 86
Sweet Potato Fries 86
Squid Rings 87
Carrot Chips 87
Corn Okra Bites 88
Salty Potato Chips 88
Corn & Beans Fries 89
Sugary Apple Fritters 89
Oregano Onion Rings 90
Chili Bacon Slices 90
Pepper Green Tomatoes 91
Avocado Sushi 91
Mayo Cauliflower Florets 92
Smoked Cashews 92
Toasted Salty Walnuts 93
Cinnamon Dough Bites 93
Salty Garlic Pretzels 94
Cinnamon Apple Rings 94
Pepper Corn Fritters 95
Cheddar Hot Dogs 95
Kale Chips 96
Coriander Shrimp Cakes 96
Crunchy Avocado Sticks 97
Pickles in Paprika 97
Bacon Eggs 98
Parmesan Zucchini Chips 98
Figs with Goat Cheese 99
Paprika Chicken Bites 99
Celery Pork Balls 100
Spinach Fritters 100
Dill Radish Fries 101
Beef Burgers 101
Cilantro Eggplant Chips 102
Chicken Mini Pies 102
Carrot & Potato Balls 103
Parmesan Chicken Sticks 103
Turmeric Carrot Balls 104
Corn Apple Tots 104
Sesame Pork Cubes 105
Parmesan Egg Clouds 105
Bacon Mozzarella 106
Creamy Salmon Pieces 106
Hot Beet Chips 107
Desserts 108
Sweet Pumpkin Loaf 108
Milky Egg Custard 109
Raisins Carrot Pie 109
Cracker Cheesecake 110
Ginger Apricot Tart 110
Banana Oatmeal Bites 111
Honey Pumpkin Delights 111
Nutmeg Blueberry Crumble 112
Cherry Crust Pie 112
Cream Cheesecake Soufflé 113
Creamy Chocolate Profiteroles 113
Oats Cookies 114
Chocolate Butter Balls 114
Apricot Cinnamon Crumble 115
Cinnamon Doughnuts 115
Raisin Vanilla Muffins 116
Chocolate Chip Muffins 116
Cocoa Brownies 117
Walnut Baked Apples 117
Nutmeg Apricot Muffins 118
Cake with Vanilla Frosting 118
Marshmallow & Butter Bananas 119
Chocolate Sauce 119
Apple Pastries 120
Cashew Cookies 120
Vanilla Oat Rolls 121
Chocolate Vanilla Soufflé 122
Almond Bars 122
Banana Pastries 123
Banana Cinnamon Cake 123
Caramel Popcorn 124
Chocolate Sugary Cupcakes 124
Cinnamon Fried Bananas 125
Marble Cocoa Cake 125
Sugary French Palmier 126
Creamy Chakali 126
Vanilla Bread Pudding 127
Oat Chocolate Chip Cookies 127

Banana Puff Rolls 128
Apple Pastry Dumplings 128
NY Cream Cheesecake 129
Cinnamon Churros 129
Banana Bread 130
Apple Pastry Roses 130
Creamy Caramel Muffins 131
Milky Semolina Cake 131
Plum Jam Tarts 132
Pumpkin Egg Mousse 132
Strawberry Cobbler 133
Vanilla Plum Crumble 133
Appendix:RecipesIndex 134

Introduction

Air fryer is a brand new kitchen appliance that can cook almost all types of food in an easier and healthier way. The process of cooking in the air fryer helps to reduce the using of oil and fats to 25 % - 30 %. It is a real super machine in comparison with other ways of cooking. The circulating hot air around the food helps to cook the meal with crispy effect. If previously, the Maillard effect was possible to get only by boiling in oil or fat – now you can cook the meal just with the small amount of it. The air fryer makes the process of cooking very suitable for people who get used to eating healthy food. Just imagine that you can cook your favorite potato chips, chicken nuggets or fish fries without any doubts about their usefulness.

The air fryer can have an adjustable temperature mode that will help you to cook the meal fast and get the desired effect. The air fryer that does not have temperature mode is also possible to use but it should have strict temperature chart. As usual, every machine has the manufacturer directions that can make the cooking process easier.

There is the wrong statement that food can be coked by itself – you should shake the ingredients during the cooking. Of course, there are some exceptions to the recipe.

Some air fryers have the food agitator – so you will not need to think about stirring the meal.

The air fryers have different sizes that can be appropriate for the various amount of people. You can choose the air fryer for a big family or that one which will be good only for two. The most recommended size of the air fryer for 2 people is 1.8 lb.

The air fryer cannot substitute you all the kitchen appliances but it can save your time and cook tasty food!

Breakfast

Broccoli Parmesan Casserole

Prep time: 10 minutes
Cooking time: 12 minutes
Servings: 2
Ingredients:

- 6 oz chicken, cooked
- 5 oz broccoli, boiled
- 2 teaspoon mayonnaise
- 1 pinch salt
- ¼ cup cream
- 3 oz Parmesan, shredded
- 1 tablespoon panko breadcrumbs
- 1 teaspoon garlic powder
- ½ teaspoon butter

Directions:

1. Preheat the air fryer to 360 F.
2. Chop the chicken and broccoli into the medium cubes.
3. Then combine mayonnaise and cream together.
4. Sprinkle the mixture with the salt, garlic powder, and butter.
5. Whisk it.
6. Place the chopped chicken in the glass form.
7. Then cover the chicken with the ½ part of all mayonnaise mixture.
8. Make the layer of the chopped broccoli and spread it with the remaining mayonnaise mixture.
9. Cover the casserole with the panko breadcrumbs.
10. Put the casserole in the air fryer and cook for 12 minutes.
11. When the casserole is cooked – serve it.
12. Enjoy!

Nutrition: calories 354, fat 16.4, fiber 2.1, carbs 11.8, protein 41.3

Chicken Sausages

Prep time: 10 minutes
Cooking time: 15 minutes
Servings: 2
Ingredients:

- 7 oz ground chicken
- ½ teaspoon chili flakes
- 1 teaspoon butter
- 1 egg
- ½ teaspoon onion powder
- ½ teaspoon garlic powder
- 1 pinch salt
- 1 pinch ground black pepper
- ½ teaspoon canola oil

Directions:

1. Put the ground chicken in the bowl.
2. Sprinkle the ground chicken with the chili flakes, butter, onion powder, garlic powder, salt, and ground black pepper.
3. Beat the egg in the ground chicken.
4. Then mix it up with the help of the fingertips.
5. When the forcemeat is cooked – make the sausages.
6. Sprinkle the sausages with the canola oil.
7. Put the air fryer to 360 F.
8. Cook the sausages for 15 minutes.
9. Turn the sausages into another part after 10 minutes of cooking.
10. Serve the sausages hot.
11. Enjoy!

Nutrition: calories 252, fat 12.6, fiber 0.1, carbs 1.2, protein 31.7

Oats Carrot Cookies

Prep time: 10 minutes
Cooking time: 8 minutes
Servings: 2
Ingredients:

- 1 carrot
- 3 tablespoon oatmeal
- 1 egg
- 1 tablespoon butter
- 2 teaspoon sugar
- ¼ teaspoon ground cinnamon
- ¼ teaspoon baking soda
- 1 tablespoon sour cream

Directions:

1. Peel the carrot and grate it.
2. Put the grated carrot in the bowl.
3. Beat the egg in the grated carrot.
4. Sprinkle the mixture with the oatmeal, butter, sugar, ground cinnamon, baking soda, and sour cream.
5. Mix it up with the help of the spoon.
6. Then make 2 big balls from the carrot mixture.
7. Flatten them gently.
8. Preheat the air fryer to 360 F.
9. Put the carrot cookies in the air fryer rack and cook them for 10 minutes.
10. When the cookies are cooked – they will be still soft.
11. Serve them warm.
12. Enjoy!

Nutrition: calories 153, fat 9.7, fiber 1.7, carbs 12.9, protein 4.3

Avocado Cheddar Rolls

Prep time: 10 minutes
Cooking time: 10 minutes
Servings: 2
Ingredients:

- ½ avocado, pitted
- 2 slices Cheddar cheese
- 4 bacon slices
- ¼ teaspoon paprika
- 1 teaspoon olive oil

Directions:

1. Peel the avocado and mash it with the help of the fork.
2. Add paprika and stir the mixture carefully.
3. After this, put 2 bacon slices beside each other and spread them with the mashed avocado.
4. Add 1 slice of Cheddar cheese and roll it.
5. Make the same steps with the remaining bacon.
6. Secure the rolls with the toothpicks. The bacon should cover all the cheese.
7. After this, preheat the air fryer to 360 F.
8. Place avocado roll in the air fryer.
9. Cook the meal for 10 minutes. Stir it once during the cooking.
10. When the rolls are cooked – serve them immediately.
11. Enjoy!

Nutrition: calories 442, fat 37.3, fiber 3.5, carbs 5.4, protein 22

Turmeric Potato Pancakes

Prep time: 10 minutes
Cooking time: 4 minutes
Servings: 2
Ingredients:

- 6 oz mashed potato
- 1 tablespoon flour
- 1 pinch salt
- 1 egg
- 1 teaspoon turmeric
- ¼ teaspoon ground thyme
- 2 oz white onion, diced
- 1 teaspoon canola oil

Directions:

1. Put the mashed potato in the bowl and crack the egg there.
2. Add salt and flour.
3. After this, sprinkle the mashed potato with the turmeric, ground thyme, and diced white onion.
4. Mix the mixture with the help of the hand mixer.
5. Then make the balls from the mashed potato mixture and flatten them with the help of the palms to get the pancake shape.
6. Preheat the air fryer to 365 F.
7. Sprinkle the air fryer basket with the canola oil inside.
8. Put the pancakes there and cook them for 4 minutes from each side.
9. When the pancakes are cooked – they will have the light brown color of the surface.
10. Enjoy the pancakes hot. Sprinkle the pancakes with the sour cream if desired.
11. Enjoy!

Nutrition: calories 178, fat 8.3, fiber 2.3, carbs 21, protein 5.3

Cheddar Eggs Burrito

Prep time: 10 minutes
Cooking time: 8 minutes
Servings: 2
Ingredients:

- 2 eggs
- ½ avocado, pitted
- ½ sweet red pepper
- 2 slices Cheddar cheese
- 1 tablespoon mayonnaise
- 1 pinch salt
- 1 pinch ground black pepper
- 1 corn tortilla

Directions:

1. Beat the eggs in the bowl and whisk them.
2. Sprinkle the whisked eggs with the salt and ground black pepper.
3. Pour the whisked egg mixture into the air fryer tray.
4. Preheat the air fryer to 365 F and put the whisked egg there.
5. Cook the eggs for 5 minutes.
6. After this, remove the cooked eggs from the air fryer.
7. Spread the corn tortilla with the mayonnaise.
8. Put the cooked eggs over the mayonnaise layer.
9. Then cut the sweet red pepper into the strips and put them on the corn tortilla too.
10. Add Cheddar cheese slices.
11. Slice the avocado and add it to the corn tortilla too.
12. After this, roll the corn tortilla to get the burrito.
13. Preheat the air fryer to 365 F.
14. Put the burrito there and cook it for 3 minutes.
15. When the burrito is cooked – remove it from the air fryer and cut into 2 parts.
16. Enjoy!

Nutrition: calories 343, fat 26.3, fiber 4.5, carbs 14.4, protein 14.5

Scrambled Eggs

Prep time: 10 minutes
Cooking time: 17 minutes
Servings: 2
Ingredients:

- 1 teaspoon butter
- 4 eggs
- ¼ teaspoon ground thyme
- 1 pinch salt
- 1 teaspoon paprika

Directions:

1. Preheat the air fryer to 345 F.
2. Toss the butter in the air fryer basket and melt it for 3 minutes.
3. Meanwhile, crack the eggs and whisk them.
4. Sprinkle the whisked eggs with the ground thyme, salt, and paprika.
5. Stir the egg mixture gently.
6. After this, pour the egg mixture into the air fryer basket.
7. Cook the eggs for 5 minutes at 345 F.
8. Then scramble the egg carefully and cook them for 5 minutes more at the same temperature.
9. After this, scramble the eggs one more time and cook at 365 F for 4 minutes more.
10. Transfer the cooked scrambled eggs in the serving plates.
11. Enjoy!

Nutrition: calories 146, fat 10.8, fiber 0.4, carbs 1.4, protein 11.3

Turkey Bread Reuben

Prep time: 10 minutes
Cooking time: 10 minutes
Servings: 2
Ingredients:

- 5 oz turkey fillet, roasted
- 4 slices grey bread
- 3 oz Swiss cheese
- 1 tablespoon mayonnaise
- 1 teaspoon pesto
- 1 teaspoon tomato sauce

Directions:

1. Slice the roasted turkey.
2. Slice Swiss cheese.
3. After this, combine the mayonnaise, pesto, and tomato sauce in the shallow bowl.
4. Stir it.
5. Spread the bread slices with the mayonnaise mixture.
6. Then put the turkey slices and cheese slices onto 2 bread slices.
7. Cover them with the 2 remaining grey bread slices.
8. Preheat the air fryer to 320 F.
9. Put the Reuben in the air fryer and cook for 10 minutes.
10. When the turkey Reuben cooked – serve the meal immediately.
11. Enjoy!

Nutrition: calories 370, fat 19.5, fiber 0.5, carbs 13.5, protein 33.9

English Eggs Bacon Breakfast

Prep time: 10 minutes
Cooking time: 16 minutes
Servings: 2
Ingredients:

- 2 slices bacon
- 2 sausages
- ¼ teaspoon salt
- ¼ teaspoon ground paprika
- 2 eggs
- 2 bread slices
- ¼ teaspoon olive oil

Directions:

1. Preheat the air fryer to 355 F.
2. Place the bacon slices and sausages on the back rack.
3. Cook the ingredients for 6 minutes.
4. After this, turn the bacon slices and sausages onto another side and cook for 7 minutes more.
5. Then transfer the cooked bacon and sausages on the serving plates.
6. After this, sprinkle the ramekins with the olive oil and beat the eggs there.
7. Cook the eggs for 3 minutes at 300 F.
8. Place the ramekins with eggs on the plate with the cooked sausages and bacon.
9. Add the bread slices.
10. Enjoy!

Nutrition: calories 240, fat 16.9, fiber 0.3, carbs 5.3, protein 15.8

Turmeric Potato

Prep time: 10 minutes
Cooking time: 25 minutes
Servings: 2
Ingredients:

- 1 teaspoon ghee
- 2 big potatoes
- 1 sweet yellow pepper
- 1 white onion, sliced
- ½ teaspoon salt
- ½ teaspoon ground black pepper
- ½ teaspoon onion powder
- ½ teaspoon turmeric

Directions:

1. Wash the potatoes carefully and cut them into the medium cubes.
2. Preheat the air fryer to 365 F.
3. Put the potato cubes in the big bowl. Add water and leave the vegetables for 10 minutes.
4. After this, drain the potatoes and dry with the help of the paper towel.
5. Place the potato cubes in the air fryer and add ghee.
6. Cook the potatoes for 15 minutes.
7. Then shake the potatoes and cook for 4 minutes more.
8. Meanwhile, remove the seeds from the sweet yellow pepper and cut it into the strips.
9. Combine the pepper strips with the sliced onion.
10. After this, combine the turmeric, onion powder, ground black pepper, and salt in the shallow bowl. Stir it gently.
11. Put the pepper-onion mixture in the air fryer.
12. Sprinkle the mixture with spices and shake gently.
13. Cook the meal for 6 minutes at 370 F.
14. Then shake the cooked meal again.
15. Enjoy!

Nutrition: calories 326, fat 2.8, fiber 11.2, carbs 70.2, protein 7.9

Milky Vanilla Toasts

Prep time: 15 minutes
Cooking time: 5 minutes
Servings: 2
Ingredients:

- 1 egg
- 4 bread slices
- 1 teaspoon vanilla extract
- 2 tablespoon milk
- 1 tablespoon sugar
- 2 teaspoon butter

Directions:

1. Beat the egg in the bowl and whisk it until smooth.
2. Then mash the butter with the help of the spoon.
3. Add the vanilla extract in the mashed butter.
4. After this, sprinkle the whisked egg with the milk and sugar. Stir it until sugar is dissolved.
5. After this, spread the bread slices with the mashed butter mixture from both sides.
6. Put the bread slices in the egg-milk mixture and let them soak all the egg liquid.
7. Preheat the air fryer to 400 F.
8. Transfer the bread slices to the air fryer rack.
9. Cook the toasts for 2 minutes from one side.
10. After this, turn the bread slices to another side and cook for 3 minutes more.
11. Cut the cooked toasts into triangles.
12. Enjoy!

Nutrition: calories 149, fat 6.9, fiber 0.4, carbs 16.3, protein 4.7

Creamy Bacon Omelet

Prep time: 10 minutes
Cooking time: 24 minutes
Servings: 2
Ingredients:

- 2 eggs
- 3 tablespoon heavy cream
- 3 bacon slices
- ¼ teaspoon oregano
- 1 pinch salt
- ¼ teaspoon cayenne pepper
- 1 teaspoon butter
- 1 oz fresh dill, chopped

Directions:

1. Crack the eggs into the mixing bowl and whisk them.
2. Then pour the heavy cream and keep whisking the mixture for 30 seconds more.
3. Preheat the air fryer to 360 F.
4. Place the bacon slices on the air fryer rack and cook it for 5 minutes from each side.
5. When the bacon is cooked – chill it little and chop.
6. Then sprinkle the egg mixture with the oregano, salt, cayenne pepper, and chopped dill.
7. Spread 2 muffin molds with the butter.
8. Pour the egg mixture there.
9. Sprinkle it with the chopped bacon.
10. Preheat the air fryer to 360 F.
11. Cook the omelet for 14 minutes.
12. When the meal is cooked – let it chill little.
13. Enjoy!

Nutrition: calories 349, fat 27.2, fiber 2.1, carbs 9.5, protein 19.5

Baked Cheddar Eggs

Prep time: 10 minutes
Cooking time: 5 minutes
Servings: 2
Ingredients:

- 2 eggs
- 2 oz ham
- 3 oz Cheddar cheese, shredded
- 1 teaspoon butter, unsalted, soft
- 1 pinch salt
- ¼ teaspoon ground chili pepper

Directions:

1. Preheat the air fryer to 360 F.
2. Take 2 ramekins and spread them with the soft butter.
3. Then slice ham and put it into the ramekins.
4. Beat the eggs into 2 ramekins.
5. Sprinkle the eggs with the salt and ground chili pepper.
6. Sprinkle the eggs with the shredded cheese.
7. Place the ramekins in the preheated air fryer and cook for 5 minutes.
8. If the eggs are not cooked enough – cook it for 1-2 minutes more.
9. Let the eggs chill for 1-2 minutes.
10. Serve and enjoy!

Nutrition: calories 297, fat 22.8, fiber 0.4, carbs 2, protein 20.9

Bacon Zucchini Boats

Prep time: 10 minutes
Cooking time: 12 minute
Servings: 2
Ingredients:

- 1 medium zucchini
- 4 bacon slices
- 1 pinch salt
- 1 pinch ground black pepper
- ½ teaspoon ground ginger
- 1 teaspoon butter

Directions:

1. Cut the zucchini crosswise to get 2 medium boards.
2. Then rub the zucchini board with the salt, ground black pepper, and ground ginger.
3. Melt the butter and brush the zucchini from each side.
4. Wrap the zucchini boards into bacon slices and secure the vegetables with the toothpicks.
5. Preheat the air fryer to 400 F.
6. Place the wrapped zucchini onto the air fryer rack and cook for 12 minutes.
7. Turn the zucchini into another side after 6 minutes of cooking.
8. When the time is over – the bacon will be a little bit crunchy.
9. Dry the zucchini boats with the paper towel.
10. Enjoy!

Nutrition: calories 240, fat 18, fiber 1.2, carbs 4.2, protein 15.3

Breakfast Parmesan Sandwich

Prep time: 10 minutes
Cooking time: 7 minutes
Servings: 2
Ingredients:

- 4 slices sandwich bread
- 1 tablespoon pesto sauce
- 1 tablespoon butter
- 4 slices Parmesan cheese
- 2 slices ham

Directions:

1. Spread two slices of the sandwich bread with the butter.
2. After this, spread another two slices of the sandwich bread with the pesto sauce.
3. Place 2 slices of Parmesan cheese and 1 slice of the ham on the sandwich bread slices.
4. Cover them with the second bread slice.
5. Preheat the air fryer to 365 F.
6. Put the sandwiches in the air fryer rack.
7. Cook the sandwiches for 7 minutes.
8. After this, chill the cooked sandwiches for 3 minutes.
9. Enjoy!

Nutrition: calories 437, fat 12.1, fiber 1.5, carbs 30.9, protein 24.6

Cheddar Baked Paprika Toasts

Prep time: 10 minutes
Cooking time: 7 minutes
Servings: 2
Ingredients:

- 2 eggs
- 2 slices, Cheddar cheese
- 2 bread slices
- 1 pinch paprika
- 1 pinch turmeric
- ½ teaspoon olive oil
- 1 tablespoon butter, salted
- 2 leaves fresh basil

Directions:

1. Sprinkle 2 ramekins with the olive oil and crack the eggs there.
2. Sprinkle the eggs with the paprika and turmeric.
3. Preheat the air fryer to 300 F.
4. Cook the eggs for 4 minutes.
5. Meanwhile, spread the bread slices with the butter.
6. When the eggs are cooked – place them over the bread layer.
7. Then place Cheddar cheese over the eggs.
8. Cook the toasts for 3 minutes at 300 F.
9. When the cheese starts to melt – the toast is cooked.
10. Serve the meal immediately.
11. Enjoy!

Nutrition: calories 152, fat 5.2, fiber 0.5, carbs 5.9, protein 6.4

Egg Ham Rolls

Prep time: 10 minutes
Cooking time: 10 minutes
Servings: 2
Ingredients:

- 1 egg, boiled
- 4 egg roll wraps
- 1 garlic clove
- ½ white onion, stewed
- 2 oz ham, chopped
- 1 teaspoon butter
- ½ teaspoon dried oregano
- 1 teaspoon olive oil

Directions:

1. Peel the boiled eggs and chop them.
2. Combine the chopped eggs with the stewed onion and ham.
3. Then peel the garlic clove and mince it.
4. Add the minced garlic in the chopped egg mixture.
5. Add dried oregano.
6. Melt butter and add it to the egg mixture too.
7. Mix the mixture up.
8. Put the egg mixture on the egg roll wraps and roll them.
9. Preheat the air fryer 380 F.
10. Place the egg rolls in the air fryer rack and spray them with the olive oil.
11. Cook the meal for 10 minutes.
12. When the egg rolls have the golden brown color – they are cooked.
13. Serve them immediately.
14. Enjoy!

Nutrition: calories 349, fat 14.2, fiber 3.4, carbs 40.9, protein 14.5

Buttery Potato Scramble

Prep time: 10 minutes
Cooking time: 25 minutes
Servings: 2
Ingredients:

- 2 medium potatoes
- 2 eggs
- 1 teaspoon butter
- ¼ teaspoon salt
- ¼ teaspoon cayenne pepper
- ½ teaspoon olive oil
- 1 teaspoon fresh dill
- 1 teaspoon fresh parsley
- 1 tablespoon soy sauce

Directions:

1. Peel the potatoes and cut them into the small cubes.
2. Sprinkle the potato cubes with the salt, soy sauce, and cayenne pepper.
3. Shake them well.
4. Preheat the air fryer to 400 F.
5. Toss the butter in the air fryer and cook for 12 minutes.
6. Meanwhile, crack the eggs into the bowl and whisk them.
7. Combine the whisked eggs with the fresh dill and fresh parsley. Stir it.
8. When the time is over – shake the potatoes well and sprinkle with the olive oil.
9. Then pour the whisked egg mixture over the potatoes and cook the meal for 3 minutes at 400 F.
10. After this, scramble the potatoes and cook for 10 minutes more at 360 F.
11. When the meal is cooked – shake it well one more time.
12. Enjoy!

Nutrition: calories 243, fat 7.7, fiber 5.3, carbs 34.9, protein 9.8

Sugary Oatmeal Muffins

Prep time: 10 minutes
Cooking time: 10 minutes
Servings: 2
Ingredients:

- ¼ cup butter
- ¼ cup powdered sugar
- 2 eggs
- 1 tablespoon flour
- 1 pinch salt
- 2 tablespoon oatmeal
- 1 teaspoon vanilla extract

Directions:

1. Melt the butter gently and combine it with the powdered sugar.
2. Start to mix the mixture using the hand mixer.
3. Beat the eggs in the separate bowl and whisk them until smooth.
4. When the butter mixture is smooth – start to add the eggs gradually.
5. Mix the butter mixture for 1 minute on the medium speed.
6. Then combine the flour and oatmeal together.
7. Add salt and stir it.
8. Add the flour mixture to the butter mixture.
9. After this, sprinkle it with the vanilla extract.
10. Knead the smooth and soft dough.
11. Preheat the air fryer to 360 F.
12. Place the dough into the muffin forms and place them in the air fryer.
13. Cook the muffins for 10 minutes.
14. Check if the muffins are cooked with the help of the toothpick.
15. Serve the muffins warm!

Nutrition: calories 364, fat 27.8, fiber 0.6, carbs 22, protein 6.9

Tofu Potato Scramble

Prep time: 15 minutes
Cooking time: 13 minutes
Servings: 2
Ingredients:

- 5 oz tofu
- 1 sweet potato
- ½ teaspoon canola oil
- 1 teaspoon soy sauce
- ¼ teaspoon garlic powder
- 1 teaspoon olive oil
- ½ teaspoon paprika
- ½ teaspoon dried oregano

Directions:

1. Cut tofu into the cubes.
2. Sprinkle tofu cubes with the canola oil and soy sauce.
3. Add garlic powder and shake tofu gently.
4. Leave tofu for 10 minutes to marinate.
5. Meanwhile, peel the sweet potato and cut it into the same cubes as tofu.
6. Sprinkle the sweet potato with the olive oil, paprika, and dried oregano,
7. Mix it up.
8. Preheat the air fryer to 400 F.
9. Put the sweet potato in the air fryer basket and cook for 8 minutes.
10. After this, add marinated tofu and cook the meal for 5 minutes more.
11. When the meal is cooked – shake it well.
12. Then transfer to the serving plates.
13. Enjoy!

Nutrition: calories 137, fat 6.7, fiber 3, carbs 14, protein 7.3

Cinnamon French Toast

Prep time: 12 minutes
Cooking time: 10 minutes
Servings: 2
Ingredients:

- 2 egg
- 4 slices white bread
- 1 tablespoon sugar
- ¼ teaspoon cinnamon
- ¼ teaspoon ground ginger
- ¼ teaspoon ground nutmeg
- 1 teaspoon vanilla extract
- 2 tablespoon milk
- 1 tablespoon maple syrup

Directions:

1. Crack the eggs into the bowl and whisk them well.
2. Then sprinkle the whisked eggs with the cinnamon, ground ginger, ground nutmeg, and vanilla extract.
3. Add milk and sugar.
4. Whisk the mixture until sugar is dissolved.
5. After this, place the bread slices in the egg mixture and leave them until they soak all the egg liquid.
6. Preheat the air fryer to 355 F.
7. Put the bread slices on the rack and cook for 10 minutes.
8. When the toasts are cooked – serve them immediately.
9. Enjoy!

Nutrition: calories 176, fat 5.4, fiber 23.7, carbs 10.8, protein 7.5

Vanilla Bread Pudding

Prep time: 15 minutes
Cooking time: 22 minutes
Servings: 2
Ingredients:

- 4 white sandwich bread slices
- 1 egg
- ¼ cup heavy cream
- 1 teaspoon vanilla extract
- 3 teaspoon butter
- ½ teaspoon ground cinnamon
- 1 tablespoon almond flakes
- 2 teaspoon raisins
- ½ teaspoon olive oil

Directions:

1. Take off the crust from the sandwich bread slices.
2. Then spread every bread slice with the butter.
3. Spray the ramekin with the olive oil.
4. Place the first bread slice in the ramekin.
5. Then sprinkle it with the vanilla extract.
6. After this, the second bread slice in the ramekin and sprinkle it with the ground cinnamon.
7. Add the third bread slice and sprinkle it with the raisins.
8. Then put the last bread slice in the ramekin.
9. Crack the egg into the bowl and whisk it.
10. Add heavy cream and whisk it.
11. Pour the egg mixture into the ramekin.
12. Sprinkle the pudding mixture with the raisins.
13. Preheat the air fryer to 360 F.
14. Put the ramekin in the air fryer and cook it for 22 minutes.
15. Serve the cooked pudding immediately.
16. Enjoy!

Nutrition: calories 300, fat 16.7, fiber 0.4, carbs 31.7, protein 7.3

Mozzarella Sausage Stromboli

Prep time: 10 minutes
Cooking time: 10 minutes
Servings: 2
Ingredients:

- 4 oz pizza crust
- 3 oz mozzarella, shredded
- 3 oz sausages, cooked, sliced
- 1 egg yolk
- ¼ teaspoon cream
- 1 teaspoon oregano

Directions:

1. Roll the pizza crust.
2. Sprinkle the pizza crust with shredded mozzarella.
3. Then add the sliced sausages and sprinkle with the oregano.
4. Roll the pizza crust and secure it in the shape of the crescent.
5. Whisk the egg yolk well and combine it with the cream. Stir it.
6. Then brush the Stromboli with the egg yolk mixture.
7. Preheat the air fryer to 370 F.
8. Put the Stromboli in the air fryer basket and cook it for 10 minutes.
9. When the Stromboli is cooked – slice it.
10. Taste it!

Nutrition: calories 433, fat 23.7, fiber 1.2, carbs 29.4, protein 26.1

Strawberry Oatmeal

Prep time: 10 minutes
Cooking time: 30 minutes
Servings: 2
Ingredients:

- ½ cup milk
- 1 egg
- 1 teaspoon vanilla extract
- 3 tablespoon brown sugar
- 6 tablespoon oatmeal
- 1 pinch salt
- 1 oz blackberry
- 1 oz strawberry
- 1 oz raspberry
- 1 pinch ground cinnamon
- 1 teaspoon honey
- 1 teaspoon butter

Directions:

1. Crack the egg into the bowl and whisk it.
2. Add the salt, vanilla extract, and milk. Stir it carefully.
3. Then combine the oatmeal and ground cinnamon together. Add the brown sugar and stir it.
4. Combine the blackberries, strawberries, and raspberries in the bowl. Shake them little.
5. Put the oatmeal in the air fryer basket.
6. Then pour the egg mixture and add berries.
7. Preheat the air fryer to 370 F and cook the meal for 30 minutes.
8. When the oatmeal is cooked – add butter and honey.
9. Mix it up and serve.
10. Enjoy!

Nutrition: calories 223, fat 6.6, fiber 3.6, carbs 34.2, protein 7.3

Cheddar Hash Browns

Prep time: 10 minutes
Cooking time: 15 minutes
Servings: 2
Ingredients:

- 2 potatoes, baked
- ¼ teaspoon garlic powder
- 3 oz. Cheddar cheese, shredded
- 1 teaspoon butter
- 1 pinch salt
- 1 pinch ground black pepper

Directions:

1. Grate the baked potatoes.
2. Preheat the air fryer to 360 F.
3. Toss the butter in the air fryer and melt it.
4. After this, reduce the temperature to 345 F.
5. Put the grated potato in the air fryer basket and cook it for 5 minutes.
6. After this, stir the grated potato carefully and sprinkle it with the garlic powder, salt, and ground black pepper.
7. Stir the mixture carefully and cook it for 5 minutes more.
8. After this, sprinkle the mixture with shredded cheese and cook it for 5 minutes at 365 F.
9. When the hash brown is cooked – stir it carefully with the help of the spatula.
10. Serve it and enjoy!

Nutrition: calories 318, fat 16.2, fiber 2.4, carbs 31.2, protein 14.2

Cheddar Bread Pizza

Prep time: 10 minutes
Cooking time: 4 minutes
Servings: 2
Ingredients:

- 1 pitta bread
- 3 oz. mozzarella cheese, shredded
- 2 oz. Cheddar cheese, shredded
- ¼ teaspoon dried oregano
- 1 teaspoon pizza sauce
- 4 slices pepperoni
- 1 teaspoon heavy cream

Directions:

1. Combine the pizza sauce, heavy cream, and dried oregano in the bowl. Whisk it.
2. Spread the pitta bread with the pizza sauce mixture.
3. Put the pepperoni over the pizza sauce mixture.
4. Then sprinkle it with the shredded mozzarella and Cheddar cheese.
5. Preheat the air fryer to 360 F and put the pizza there.
6. Cook it for 4 minutes.
7. When the breakfast pizza is cooked – serve it immediately.
8. Enjoy!

Nutrition: calories 370, fat 23, fiber 0.7, carbs 16.3, protein 23.9

Mozzarella Pepperoni Patties

Prep time: 10 minutes
Cooking time: 5 minutes
Servings: 2
Ingredients:

- 4 thick mozzarella slices
- 4 pepperoni slices
- 3 tablespoon panko breadcrumbs
- 1 egg
- 3 tablespoon flour
- ¼ teaspoon dried rosemary
- 1 pinch salt

Directions:

1. Place the pepperoni slices on two mozzarella slices.
2. Then cover the mozzarella slices with the remaining cheese to make the cheese sandwiches.
3. Beat the egg in the bowl and whisk it.
4. Then sprinkle the mozzarella sandwiches with the flour and dip them in the whisked egg.
5. Sprinkle Mozzarella patties with the panko breadcrumbs.
6. Preheat the air fryer to 400 F.
7. Put the patties in the air fryer basket and cook them for 5 minutes.
8. Flip them after 2 minutes of cooking.
9. Serve the patties immediately.
10. Enjoy!

Nutrition: calories 329, fat 17.7, fiber 0.8, carbs 18.5, protein 23.8

Paprika Soufflé

Prep time: 5 minutes
Cooking time: 5 minutes
Servings: 2
Ingredients:

- 3 eggs
- 2 tablespoon heavy cream
- 1 pinch salt
- ¼ teaspoon paprika
- ¼ teaspoon ground turmeric

Directions:

1. Preheat the air fryer to 360 F.
2. Crack the eggs into the bowl and whisk them.
3. Add the heavy cream.
4. Then sprinkle the egg mixture with the salt, paprika, and ground turmeric.
5. Stir it carefully.
6. Pour the egg mixture into 2 ramekins.
7. Put the ramekins in the air fryer basket and cook the soufflé for 5 minutes.
8. When the soufflé is cooked – chill it for 3 minutes.
9. Enjoy!

Nutrition: calories 148, fat 12.2, fiber 0.2, carbs 1.3, protein 8.7

Tabasco Chicken Meatballs

Prep time: 10 minutes
Cooking time: 15 minutes
Servings: 2
Ingredients:

- 1 tablespoon chives
- 1 teaspoon Tabasco
- 5 oz. ground chicken
- 3 oz. ground pork
- ¼ teaspoon minced garlic
- ¼ teaspoon onion powder
- 1 teaspoon semolina
- 1 teaspoon olive oil

Directions:

1. Take the big bowl and put the ground chicken, ground pork, minced garlic, onion powder, and semolina.
2. Add chives and Tabasco.
3. Stir it carefully.
4. Then make the small meatballs.
5. Preheat the air fryer to 360 F and put the meatballs in the air fryer basket.
6. Cook the meatballs for 15 minutes.
7. When the meatballs are cooked – let them chill gently.
8. Enjoy!

Nutrition: calories 224, fat 9.1, fiber 0.2, carbs 1.7, protein 32

Cheddar Zucchini Frittata

Prep time: 10 minutes
Cooking time: 18 minutes
Servings: 2
Ingredients:

- 1 zucchini
- 3 oz. Cheddar cheese, shredded
- 1 pinch salt
- ½ white onion, diced
- 2 eggs
- 2 tablespoon milk
- ¼ teaspoon paprika
- ¼ teaspoon butter

Directions:

1. Cut the zucchini into the strips and combine it with the diced onion.
2. Preheat the air fryer to 360 F and toss butter there.
3. When the butter is melted – put the zucchini mixture in the air fryer basket.
4. Cook the zucchini mixture for 8 minutes.
5. Meanwhile, beat the eggs in the bowl and whisk them.
6. Add the salt, paprika, and milk. Stir it.
7. When the time is over – pour the egg mixture into the air fryer and stir it.
8. Cook the frittata for 5 minutes at 360 F.
9. Then add the shredded cheese and cook it for 5 minutes more at 370 F.
10. Serve the cooked frittata immediately.
11. Enjoy!

Nutrition: calories 274, fat 19.5, fiber 1.8, carbs 7.6, protein 18.2

Milky Cod

Prep time: 10 minutes
Cooking time: 13 minutes
Servings: 2
Ingredients:

- 10 oz. cod fillet
- ¼ cup breadcrumbs
- 1 egg
- ¼ cup milk
- 1 pinch salt
- ½ teaspoon ground black pepper
- ½ teaspoon olive oil
- 1 teaspoon dried cilantro

Directions:

1. Cut the cod fillet into servings.
2. Then beat the egg into the bowl and whisk it.
3. Add the milk and whisk it for 10 seconds more.
4. After this, sprinkle the cod fillets with the salt, ground black pepper, and dried cilantro.
5. Put the cod fillets in the egg mixture and then coat them with the breadcrumbs.
6. Preheat the air fryer to 360 F.
7. Put the cod fillets in the air fryer and cook the fish for 13 minutes.
8. Serve the crumbed fish immediately.
9. Enjoy!

Nutrition: calories 225, fat 6, fiber 0.8, carbs 11.7, protein 30.9

Chicken Mushroom Rolls

Prep time: 10 minutes
Cooking time: 5 minutes
Servings: 2
Ingredients:

- 2 spring roll wraps
- 7 oz. chicken breast, cooked
- 1 egg
- 2 oz. carrot
- 2 oz. mushroom
- 1 oz. onion, diced
- 1 teaspoon chives

Directions:

1. Shred the cooked chicken breast.
2. Cut the carrot into the strips.
3. Slice the mushrooms.
4. Combine the shredded chicken breast, carrot strips, and sliced mushrooms in the bowl.
5. Add diced onion and chives.
6. Stir the mixture carefully.
7. Then place the chicken filling into the roll wraps and roll them.
8. Beat the egg in the bowl and whisk it.
9. Seal the spring rolls with the help of the whisked egg.
10. Preheat the air fryer to 360 F.
11. Cook the spring rolls for 5 minutes.
12. When the meal is cooked – serve it immediately.
13. Enjoy!

Nutrition: calories 168, fat 4.8, fiber 1.3, carbs 5.2, protein 25.1

Running Cheddar Eggs

Prep time: 5 minutes
Cooking time: 6 minutes
Servings: 2
Ingredients:

- 4 eggs
- 1 pinch salt
- 3 oz. cheddar cheese, shredded
- 1 tablespoon dill, chopped
- ¼ teaspoon butter

Directions:

1. Preheat the air fryer to 360 F.
2. Toss the butter in the air fryer and melt it.
3. Beat the eggs in the melted butter.
4. Sprinkle the eggs with the salt and chopped dill.
5. Cook the eggs for 4 minutes.
6. After this, sprinkle the eggs with the shredded cheese and cook them for 2 minutes more.
7. Transfer the cooked eggs to the serving plates.
8. Enjoy!

Nutrition: calories 305, fat 23.4, fiber 0.2, carbs 2.1, protein 22

Cheddar Potato Halves

Prep time: 15 minutes
Cooking time: 18 minutes
Servings: 2
Ingredients:

- 2 potatoes
- 1 teaspoon scallion, chopped
- ¼ teaspoon butter
- 3 oz. Cheddar cheese, shredded
- 3 oz. ground chicken
- 1 teaspoon tomato sauce
- 1 pinch salt
- 1 pinch ground black pepper

Directions:

1. Wash the potatoes carefully and cut them into the halves.
2. Combine the chopped scallions, shredded cheese, ground chicken, tomato sauce, salt, and ground black pepper.
3. Mix the mixture up.
4. After this, remove the flesh from the potato halves and chop it.
5. Combine the potato flesh with the ground chicken mixture.
6. Then fill the potato halves with the chicken mixture.
7. Put the small piece of the butter over every potato halve.
8. Preheat the air fryer to 400 F.
9. Put the potato halves in the air fryer basket and cook them for 18 minutes.
10. When the potato halves are cooked – the filling should be very soft.
11. Serve the cooked meal immediately.
12. Enjoy!

Nutrition: calories 404, fat 17.9, fiber 5.2, carbs 34.2, protein 26.5

Chicken Strips

Prep time: 10 minutes
Cooking time: 20 minutes
Servings: 2
Ingredients:

- 11 oz. chicken fillet
- ¼ teaspoon salt
- ¼ teaspoon dried oregano
- ¼ teaspoon paprika
- ¼ teaspoon turmeric
- 2 tablespoon breadcrumbs
- ¼ teaspoon ground black pepper
- 1 teaspoon olive oil
- 1 teaspoon sour cream

Directions:

1. Cut the chicken fillet into the medium strips.
2. Then combine the salt, dried oregano, paprika, turmeric, and ground black pepper in the bowl.
3. Shake it gently to make the homogeneous texture.
4. Then coat the chicken strips with the spice mixture.
5. Combine the sour cream and olive oil together. Whisk it.
6. Sprinkle the chicken strips with the sour cream mixture gently.
7. Then sprinkle the chicken strips with the breadcrumbs.
8. Preheat the air fryer to 360 F.
9. Put the chicken strips in the air fryer basket and cook for 20 minutes.
10. When the chicken strips are cooked – let them chill and serve.
11. Enjoy!

Nutrition: calories 350, fat 14.8, fiber 0.6, carbs 5.6, protein 46.2

Wrapped Bacon Eggs

Prep time: 8 minutes
Cooking time: 10 minutes
Servings: 2
Ingredients:

- 4 eggs, boiled
- 4 bacon slices
- 1 pinch salt
- 1 pinch cayenne pepper
- 1 pinch paprika
- ½ teaspoon canola oil

Directions:

1. Peel the boiled eggs.
2. Sprinkle the bacon slices with the salt, cayenne pepper, and paprika.
3. Preheat the air fryer to 360 F.
4. Put the bacon slices in the air fryer rack and cook for 5 minutes.
5. After this, chill the bacon.
6. Wrap the peeled eggs in the bacon slices and secure them gently with the toothpicks.
7. After this, put the wrapped eggs in the air fryer basket and sprinkle with the canola oil.
8. Cook the bacon eggs for 5 minutes more.
9. The eggs are cooked – when the surface of the bacon is a little bit crunchy – the meal is cooked.
10. Serve it!

Nutrition: calories 342, fat 25.8, fiber 0.1, carbs 1.4, protein 25.2

Banana Pancakes

Prep time: 8 minutes
Cooking time: 10 minutes
Servings: 2
Ingredients:

- 1 teaspoon flour
- 1 banana
- 1 egg
- ¼ teaspoon ground cinnamon
- 2 teaspoon maple syrup
- 1/3 teaspoon vanilla extract

Directions:

1. Beat the egg in the bowl.
2. Peel the banana and add it to the egg bowl.
3. Mash the egg mixture with the help of the fork.
4. When the mixture is homogenous – add flour and vanilla extract. Mix it up with the help of the hand mixer.
5. Preheat the air fryer to 300 F.
6. Separate the banana mixture into 2 parts.
7. Pour the first part of the banana mixture in the air fryer.
8. Cook it for 5 minutes.
9. When the pancake is cooked – transfer it to the serving plate.
10. Cook the remaining banana mixture.
11. When 2 pancakes are cooked – serve them with the maple syrup.
12. Enjoy!

Nutrition: calories 109, fat 2.4, fiber 1.7, carbs 19.4, protein 3.6

Honey Pumpkin Mash

Prep time: 15 minutes
Cooking time: 11 minutes
Servings: 2
Ingredients:

- 1 tablespoon honey
- ½ teaspoon ground cinnamon
- ¼ teaspoon ground ginger
- 10 oz. pumpkin
- ¼ teaspoon butter
- 1 teaspoon heavy cream

Directions:

1. Peel the pumpkin and cut it into the cubes.
2. Sprinkle the pumpkin cubes with the honey and ground cinnamon.
3. Then add ground ginger and shake it.
4. Melt the butter and combine it with the heavy cream. Stir it.
5. Leave the pumpkin cubes for 10 minutes to let it gives the juice.
6. Preheat the air fryer to 400 F.
7. Put the juicy pumpkin mixture in the air fryer and cook it for 11 minutes.
8. When the pumpkin is soft – it is cooked.
9. Blend the pumpkin with the help of the hand blender.
10. Then add the melted heavy cream mixture and stir it carefully.
11. Serve the pumpkin mash immediately.
12. Enjoy!

Nutrition: calories 95, fat 1.8, fiber 4.5, carbs 20.8, protein 1.7

Cheese Oatmeal Fritters

Prep time: 10 minutes
Cooking time: 4 minutes
Servings: 2
Ingredients:

- 1 egg
- 10 oz. cottage cheese
- 1 teaspoon semolina
- 1 tablespoon sour cream
- 1 tablespoon brown sugar
- 1 teaspoon oatmeal
- ½ teaspoon vanilla extract
- ½ teaspoon olive oil

Directions:

1. Mash the cottage cheese with the help of the fork.
2. Beat the egg in the mixture and stir it until homogenous.
3. Add semolina, sour cream, brown sugar, oatmeal, and vanilla extract.
4. Mix it up.
5. Then form the medium fritters from the mixture.
6. Preheat the air fryer to 360 F.
7. Spray the air fryer basket with the olive oil inside.
8. Then put the cottage cheese fritters.
9. Cook the fritters for 2 minutes from each side.
10. When the fritters are cooked – chill for 1 minute.
11. Serve the fritters. Sprinkle the meal with the liquid honey if desired.
12. Enjoy!

Nutrition: calories 211, fat 7.4, fiber 0.2, carbs 12, protein 22.8

Parmesan Spinach Quiche

Prep time: 15 minutes
Cooking time: 15 minutes
Servings: 2
Ingredients:

- 3 oz. fresh spinach
- 1 egg
- 1 teaspoon cream
- 4 tablespoon flour
- 1 pinch salt
- 1 tablespoon butter
- 3 oz. Parmesan, shredded
- ½ teaspoon dried dill

Directions:

1. Combine the salt, butter, and flour together.
2. Knead the non-sticky dough.
3. Roll the dough with the help of the rolling pin.
4. Then place the rolled dough in the air fryer form.
5. Beat the egg in the bowl and whisk it.
6. Add cream and dried dill.
7. Stir it.
8. Pour the egg mixture into the quiche crust.
9. Chop the fresh spinach and put it in the quiche crust.
10. Preheat the air fryer to 350 F and put the quiche there.
11. Cook the meal for 10 minutes.
12. After this, sprinkle it with the shredded cheese.
13. Reduce the temperature to 345 F and cook the quiche for 5 minutes more.
14. Then chill the cooked quiche and serve it.
15. Enjoy!

Nutrition: calories 406, fat 21, fiber 1.4, carbs 32, protein 20.7

Egg Sandwich

Prep time: 10 minutes
Cooking time: 7 minutes
Servings: 2
Ingredients:

- 4 slices of sandwich bread
- 4 eggs
- 1 pinch salt
- 1 teaspoon dried dill
- ¼ teaspoon dried oregano
- 1 teaspoon butter

Directions:

1. Make the holes in the sandwich bread slices.
2. Preheat the air fryer to 360 F.
3. Melt the butter and put the bread slices in the air fryer basket.
4. Then beat the eggs in the bread holes.
5. Sprinkle the eggs with the dried dill, salt, and dried oregano.
6. Cook the eggs in holes for 5 minutes.
7. After this, turn the eggs into holes to another side and cook for 2 minutes more.
8. Serve the cooked meal hot.
9. Enjoy!

Nutrition: calories 285, fat 12.7, fiber 1.2, carbs 29.1, protein 15.2

Eggs in Bacon Cups

Prep time: 10 minutes
Cooking time: 12 minutes
Servings: 2
Ingredients:

- 1 tablespoon scallions, chopped
- 1 pinch salt
- 2 eggs
- 6 bacon slices
- ¼ teaspoon chili flakes
- 1 teaspoon butter

Directions:

1. Preheat the air fryer to 360 F.
2. Take the muffin molds and put the better there.
3. After this, place 3 bacon slices in every mold.
4. Then beat the eggs in the molds.
5. Sprinkle the eggs with the chopped scallions and salt.
6. Add chili flakes.
7. Put the bacon cups in the air fryer and cook them for 12 minutes.
8. When the eggs are cooked – let them chill little.
9. Discard the bacon cups from the muffin molds and serve them.
10. Enjoy!

Nutrition: calories 389, fat 30.1, fiber 0.1, carbs 1.4, protein 26.7

Leek Parmesan Tarts

Prep time: 10 minutes
Cooking time: 10 minutes
Servings: 2
Ingredients:

- 4 oz. puff pastry
- 1 egg yolk
- ¼ teaspoon ground black pepper
- ¼ teaspoon chili flakes
- 3 oz. Parmesan, shredded
- 1 pinch salt
- 3 oz. leek
- ½ teaspoon butter
- 1 teaspoon cream

Directions:

1. Roll the puff pastry.
2. Whisk the egg yolk.
3. Brush the puff pastry with the whisked egg yolk.
4. After this, sprinkle the puff pastry with the shredded cheese.
5. Then sprinkle the ground black pepper, chili flakes, and salt over the shredded cheese.
6. Chop the leek and combine it with the cream.
7. Stir it.
8. Melt butter.
9. Place the chopped leek over the cheese and sprinkle with the butter.
10. Preheat the air fryer to 400 F.
11. Cut the tart into 2 parts and place them in the air fryer.
12. Cook the tarts for 10 minutes.
13. When the meal is cooked – let it chill little.
14. Serve it!

Nutrition: calories 512, fat 34.2, fiber 1.7, carbs 33.7, protein 19.9

Avocado Eggs

Prep time: 10 minutes
Cooking time: 7 minutes
Servings: 2

- **Ingredients** 1 avocado, pitted
- 2 eggs
- 1 pinch ground black pepper
- ¼ teaspoon fresh parsley, chopped
- ¼ teaspoon chives

Directions:

1. Cut the avocado into the halves.
2. Sprinkle the avocado halves with the ground black pepper and chives.
3. Then beat the eggs into the avocado halves.
4. Preheat the air fryer to 360 F.
5. Put the avocado eggs in the air fryer basket and cook them for 7 minutes.
6. When the meal is cooked – sprinkle it with the chopped fresh parsley.
7. Serve it immediately.
8. Enjoy!

Nutrition: calories 268, fat 24, fiber 6.8, carbs 9, protein 7.5

Smoked Salmon Omelet

Prep time: 10 minutes
Cooking time: 8 minutes
Servings: 2

- **Ingredients** 3 oz. smoked salmon, chopped
- 4 eggs
- 1 teaspoon scallions
- 1 pinch salt
- ¼ teaspoon ground black pepper
- ¼ teaspoon chili flakes
- ½ teaspoon butter
- 2 tablespoon cream

Directions:

1. Beat the eggs in the bowl and whisk them.
2. Add the scallions and salt.
3. After this, sprinkle the eggs with the ground black pepper, chili flakes, and cream.
4. Stir it carefully.
5. Preheat the air fryer to 360 F.
6. Toss the butter in the air fryer basket and melt it.
7. After this, pour the egg mixture into the melted butter.
8. Add the chopped smoked salmon.
9. Cook the omelet for 8 minutes.
10. Transfer the cooked omelet onto the serving plates.
11. Enjoy!

Nutrition: calories193, fat 12.2, fiber 0.1, carbs 1.3, protein 19

Paprika Chicken Buns

Prep time: 10 minutes
Cooking time: 12 minutes
Servings: 2

- **Ingredients** 6 oz. ground chicken
- ¼ teaspoon minced garlic
- ¼ teaspoon ground black pepper
- 1 pinch salt
- ¼ teaspoon paprika
- 4 oz. puff pastry
- ½ teaspoon butter
- 1 tablespoon water

Directions:

1. Roll the puff pastry.
2. Combine the ground chicken with the minced garlic, ground black pepper, salt, paprika, and butter.
3. Mix the mixture up.
4. After this, cut the puff pastry into 4 squares.
5. Put the ground chicken mixture in the center of every puff pastry square.
6. Secure the edges of the dough to make the shape of the bun.
7. Preheat the air fryer to 370 F.
8. Sprinkle the buns with water and place them in the air fryer basket.
9. Cook the chicken buns for 12 minutes.
10. When the buns are cooked – let them chill little.
11. Enjoy!

Nutrition: calories 484, fat 28.9, fiber 1, carbs 26, protein 28.8

Parmesan Chorizo Rolls

Prep time: 10 minutes
Cooking time: 11 minutes
Servings: 2

- **Ingredients** 3 oz puff pastry
- 3 oz chorizo
- 1 tablespoon fresh parsley
- 1 teaspoon tomato sauce
- 2 oz Parmesan, shredded
- 1 teaspoon butter
- ¼ teaspoon ground thyme

Directions:

1. Roll the puff pastry
2. Spread it with the tomato sauce and sprinkle it with the shredded cheese.
3. Then chop the fresh parsley put it over the cheese.
4. After this, sprinkle the dough with the ground thyme.
5. Chop the chorizo and add it to the dough too.
6. Roll the dough and cut it into 4 small rolls.
7. Melt the butter.
8. Brush the rolls with the butter.
9. Preheat the air fryer to 365 F.
10. Put the chorizo rolls on the air fryer rack and cook them for 11 minutes.
11. When the meal is cooked – serve it immediately.
12. Enjoy!

Nutrition: calories 537, fat 40.5, fiber 0.8, carbs 21.3, protein 22.6

Cheddar Crumpets

Prep time: 25 minutes
Cooking time: 12 minutes
Servings: 2
Ingredients:

- 2 oz. Queso Fresco
- 2 tablespoon milk
- 3 tablespoon flour
- ¼ teaspoon sugar
- 1 pinch dried yeast
- ¼ teaspoon butter
- 2 oz. Cheddar cheese, shredded

Directions:

1. Melt Queso Fresco and preheat the milk.
2. Combine the ingredients together and stir until you get the smooth mixture.
3. Then combine flour, sugar, and yeast in the bowl.
4. Start to add the milk mixture gradually.
5. Stir it constantly.
6. Leave the mixture for 10 minutes at the warm place.
7. After this, add shredded Cheddar cheese and stir it.
8. Melt the butter and add it to the dough too.
9. Stir it well and leave it for 5 minutes more.
10. Then pour the smooth dough into the ramekins.
11. Preheat the air fryer to 370 F.
12. Put the ramekins in the air fryer basket and cook for 12 minutes.
13. When the crumpets are cooked – they will be still soft but with the crunchy surface.
14. Let the crumpets chill little.
15. Serve and enjoy!

Nutrition: calories 209, fat 12.7, fiber 0.4, carbs 10.7, protein 12.7

Main Dishes

Pork Strips

Prep time: 18 minutes
Cooking time: 10 minutes
Servings: 2
Ingredients

- 15 oz pork fillet
- 1 teaspoon sesame seeds
- 1 teaspoon sesame oil
- 1 teaspoon apple cider vinegar
- 1 teaspoon soy sauce
- 1 teaspoon scallions, chopped
- ½ teaspoon ground black pepper

Directions:

1. Cut the pork fillet into the strips.
2. Put the pork strips in the bowl and sprinkle them with the sesame oil, apple cider vinegar, soy sauce, and ground black pepper.
3. Mix the meat gently and leave it for 10 minutes.
4. Preheat the air fryer to 400 F.
5. Put the pork strips in the air fryer basket and cook for 10 minutes.
6. Shake the pork strips after 6 minutes of cooking.
7. When the pork strips are cooked – sprinkle them with the chopped scallions and serve.
8. Enjoy!

Nutrition: calories 528, fat 30, fiber 0.4, carbs 1, protein 59.7

Pineapple Chicken Breast

Prep time: 15 minutes
Cooking time: 25 minutes
Servings: 2
Ingredients

- 2 teaspoon pineapple, canned
- 12 oz chicken breast
- 1 teaspoon butter
- ¼ teaspoon ground black pepper
- ½ teaspoon olive oil
- 1 tablespoon mayonnaise
- ¼ teaspoon chili flakes

Directions:

1. Make the cut in the chicken breast crosswise.
2. Sprinkle the chicken breast with the ground black pepper, mayonnaise, and chili flakes.
3. Stir the chicken breast carefully.
4. After this, sprinkle the chicken breast with the olive oil.
5. Chop the pineapple into the tiny pieces.
6. Fill the chicken breast with the chopped pineapple.
7. Add butter and secure the chicken breast with the toothpicks.
8. Preheat the air fryer to 360 F and put the chicken breast in the air fryer basket.
9. Cook the chicken breast for 25 minutes.
10. When the meal is cooked – let it chill little and slice.
11. Enjoy!

Nutrition: calories 252, fat 9.8, fiber 0.1, carbs 2.4, protein 36.2

Catfish Nuggets

Prep time: 10 minutes
Cooking time: 8 minutes
Servings: 2
Ingredients

- ½ cup breadcrumbs
- 1 egg
- 12 oz catfish fillet
- ¼ teaspoon salt
- 2 tablespoon cream
- 1 teaspoon olive oil
- 1 teaspoon dried cilantro

Directions:

1. Crack the egg into the bowl and whisk it.
2. Add cream and stir the egg mixture carefully.
3. After this, cut the catfish fillet into medium pieces.
4. Sprinkle the catfish pieces with the salt and dried oregano.
5. Then dip the fish pieces into the egg mixture.
6. After this, coat the fish pieces in the bread crumbs.
7. Preheat the air fryer to 400 F.
8. Put the chicken nuggets onto the air fryer tray and spray them with the olive oil.
9. Cook the fish nuggets for 8 minutes.
10. Flip the fish nuggets into another side after 4 minutes of cooking.
11. The cooked nuggets will be crunchy.
12. Enjoy!

Nutrition: calories 396, fat 19.5, fiber 1.2, carbs 20, protein 32.9

Creamy Coriander Tilapia

Prep time: 12 minutes
Cooking time: 16 minutes
Servings: 2
Ingredients

- ¼ cup cream
- 15 oz tilapia fillet
- ½ teaspoon garlic, sliced
- ¼ teaspoon ground coriander
- 1 teaspoon fresh thyme
- ½ teaspoon butter

Directions:

1. Put the tilapia fillet in the bowl.
2. Sprinkle it with the sliced garlic, ground coriander, and fresh thyme.
3. Add cream and stir the fish well.
4. Preheat the air fryer to 360 F.
5. Toss the butter in the air fryer basket and melt it.
6. Then put the tilapia fillet in the melted butter.
7. Sprinkle it with the remaining cream mixture and cook for 16 minutes.
8. Flip the tilapia fillet into another side after 8 minutes of cooking.
9. Transfer the cooked tilapia to the serving plate.
10. Enjoy!

Nutrition: calories 205, fat 4.6, fiber 0.2, carbs 1.5, protein 39.9

Italian Beer Cod

Prep time: 20 minutes
Cooking time: 10 minutes
Servings: 2
Ingredients

- ½ cup beer
- ¼ teaspoon salt
- ½ teaspoon ground black pepper
- 14 oz cod fillet
- 4 tablespoon breadcrumbs
- 1 tablespoon Italian seasoning
- ½ teaspoon olive oil
- 1 egg

Directions:

1. Sprinkle the cod fillet with the salt and ground black pepper.
2. Then put the cod fillet in the beer and leave it for 10 minutes.
3. Meanwhile, combine the breadcrumbs and Italian seasoning in the bowl. Stir the mixture.
4. Crack the egg into the bowl and whisk it.
5. Remove the fish fillet from the beer and cut it into 2 parts.
6. Then dip the fish pieces into the egg mixture.
7. After this, sprinkle the fish pieces with the breadcrumb mixture.
8. Preheat the air fryer to 400 F.
9. Put the fish pieces in the air fryer tray and sprinkle them with the olive oil.
10. Cook the fish fillet for 4 minutes.
11. After this, flip the fish fillets to another side and cook them for 6 minutes.
12. Serve the cooked fish immediately.
13. Enjoy!

Nutrition: calories 264, fat 7.5, fiber 0.8, carbs 13.1, protein 31.7

Garlic Catfish

Prep time: 18 minutes
Cooking time: 9 minutes
Servings: 2
Ingredients

- 14 oz catfish
- 2 teaspoon minced garlic
- 1 teaspoon olive oil
- ½ teaspoon butter
- ½ teaspoon dried dill
- ½ teaspoon dried parsley
- 1 teaspoon onion powder
- ½ teaspoon garlic powder

Directions:

1. Rub the catfish with the minced garlic.
2. Then combine the olive oil with the dried dill, dried parsley, onion powder, and garlic powder.
3. Whisk it until homogenous.
4. Then brush the catfish with the oil mixture.
5. Leave the catfish for 10 minutes to marinate.
6. Preheat the air fryer to 400 F.
7. Melt the butter in the air fryer and put the catfish there.
8. Cook the catfish for 6 minutes.
9. After this, flip the fish to another side and cook for 3 minutes more.
10. When the fish is cooked – let it chill briefly.
11. Enjoy!

Nutrition: calories 494, fat 29.8, fiber 1.6, carbs 18.5, protein 36.4

Turmeric Snapper

Prep time: 20 minutes
Cooking time: 12 minutes
Servings: 2
Ingredients

- 12 oz snapper
- ½ lemon
- 2 garlic cloves
- ½ yellow onion
- ¼ teaspoon ground thyme
- ¼ teaspoon turmeric
- ½ teaspoon dried dill
- 1 tablespoon fresh parsley
- 1 teaspoon olive oil
- 1 teaspoon butter

Directions:

1. Slice the lemon.
2. Dice the yellow onion and chop the garlic cloves.
3. Rub the snapper with the ground thyme, turmeric, dried dill, and olive oil.
4. Massage the fish gently.
5. After this, fill the snapper with the fresh dill and better.
6. Make the small cuts on the surface of the fish and put the sliced lemon into the cuts.
7. Preheat the air fryer to 365 F.
8. Put the snapper in the air fryer basket and cook the fish for 12 minutes.
9. Check if the fish is cooked and discard it from the air fryer basket.
10. After this, cut the fish into 2 servings.
11. Enjoy!

Nutrition: calories 279, fat 7.4, fiber 1.3, carbs 5.4, protein 44.8

Orange Beef Mignon

Prep time: 30 minutes
Cooking time: 18 minutes
Servings: 2
Ingredients

- 15 oz beef mignon
- 1 orange
- ½ teaspoon white pepper
- ½ teaspoon ground black pepper
- 1 teaspoon olive oil
- ¼ teaspoon ground thyme
- ¼ teaspoon dried cilantro

Directions:

1. Grate the zest from the orange.
2. After this, squeeze juice from the orange.
3. Cut the beef into 2 servings.
4. Combine the orange juice, orange zest, white pepper, ground black pepper, olive oil, ground thyme, and dried cilantro.
5. Mix it and dip the beef there.
6. Leave the beef for 20 minutes to marinate in the fridge.
7. Preheat the air fryer to 400 F.
8. Put the beef mignons in the air fryer and sprinkle with ½ part of orange juice mixture.
9. Cook the meat for 18 minutes.
10. When the beef mignon is cooked – transfer the meal to the serving plates.
11. Taste it.

Nutrition: calories 380, fat 17.2, fiber 2.4, carbs 11.2, protein 42

Chicken Oatmeal Schnitzel

Prep time: 10 minutes
Cooking time: 13 minutes
Servings: 2
Ingredients

- 2 chicken fillets
- ½ teaspoon salt
- ½ teaspoon ground black pepper
- 1 egg
- ¼ cup oatmeal flour
- ½ teaspoon olive oil

Directions:

1. Beat the chicken fillets well.
2. Then sprinkle the chicken fillets with the salt and ground black pepper from each side.
3. Crack the egg into the bowl and whisk it.
4. Dip the chicken fillets in the whisked egg.
5. Then coat the chicken in the oatmeal flour.
6. Preheat the air fryer to 355 F.
7. Put the chicken fillets on the air fryer tray and spray them with the olive oil.
8. Cook the schnitzels for 13 minutes.
9. Flip the chicken to another side after 6 minutes of cooking.
10. Serve the cooked schnitzels hot.
11. Enjoy!

Nutrition: calories 303, fat 14.9, fiber 2, carbs 20.6, protein 23.2

Salty Pork Belly

Prep time: 10 minutes
Cooking time: 30 minutes
Servings: 2
Ingredients

- 9 oz pork belly
- 1 teaspoon salt
- 2 tablespoon olive oil
- ½ teaspoon ground black pepper

Directions:

1. Sprinkle the pork belly with the salt and ground black pepper.
2. After this, brush the pork belly with the olive oil.
3. Preheat the air fryer to 320 F.
4. Put the pork belly there and cook it for 20 minutes.
5. After this, increase the temperature to 360 F and cook it for 10 minutes more.
6. Let the cooked pork belly chill till the room temperature.
7. Taste it!

Nutrition: calories 710, fat 48.4, fiber 0.1, carbs 0.3, protein 58.9

Ribeye Beef Steak

Prep time: 10 minutes
Cooking time: 20 minutes
Servings: 2
Ingredients

- 2 ribeye steak
- 1 teaspoon paprika
- ½ teaspoon ground black pepper
- ½ teaspoon salt
- 1 teaspoon rosemary
- 1 tablespoon Mustard
- 1 teaspoon mayonnaise
- 1 teaspoon olive oil

Directions:

1. Rub the ribeye steaks with the paprika, ground black pepper, salt, rosemary, Mustard, and mayonnaise.
2. Mix the ribeye steaks carefully.
3. After this, sprinkle the meat with the olive oil.
4. Preheat the air fryer to 400 F.
5. Put the ribeye steaks in the air fryer basket and cook for 12 minutes.
6. Then flip the ribeye steaks to another side and cook for 8 minutes more at the same temperature.
7. Transfer the cooked meal to the serving plates.
8. Enjoy!

Nutrition: calories 736, fat 35.5, fiber 1.6, carbs 3.9, protein 97.4

Garlic Ground Chicken

Prep time: 10 minutes
Cooking time: 10 minutes
Servings: 2
Ingredients

- 12 oz ground chicken
- 1 teaspoon minced garlic
- ½ teaspoon onion, grated
- ¼ teaspoon chili flakes
- ½ teaspoon white pepper
- 1 teaspoon butter
- 1 tablespoon fresh parsley, chopped

Directions:

1. Take the air fryer tray and put butter there.
2. Preheat the air fryer to 365 F and melt the butter.
3. After this, put the ground chicken in the melted butter.
4. Sprinkle the meat with the minced garlic, grated onion, chili flakes, and white pepper.
5. Stir it and cook the meal for 8 minutes.
6. After this, stir this meal and sprinkle it with the chopped fresh parsley.
7. Stir the mixture and cook it for 3 minutes at 400 F.
8. When the meal is cooked – transfer it to the serving plates.
9. Enjoy!

Nutrition: calories 345, fat 14.6, fiber 0.3, carbs 1, protein 49.5

Pork Chops

Prep time: 10 minutes
Cooking time: 20 minutes
Servings: 2
Ingredients

- 2 pork chops
- ½ teaspoon minced garlic
- ¼ teaspoon ground black pepper
- 1/3 teaspoon salt
- ¼ teaspoon ground paprika

Directions:

1. Beat the pork chops gently.
2. After this, combine the ground black pepper, salt, and ground paprika in the bowl.
3. Shake it to make homogeneous.
4. Then rub the pork chops with the minced garlic from both sides.
5. Then sprinkle the pork chops with the spices.
6. Preheat the air fryer to 360 F.
7. Cook the pork chops for 20 minutes.
8. When the time is over – remove the pork chops from the air fryer and serve them.
9. Enjoy!

Nutrition: calories 258, fat 19.9, fiber 0.2, carbs 0.5, protein 18.1

Crunchy Catfish

Prep time: 10 minutes
Cooking time: 10 minutes
Servings: 2
Ingredients

- 12 oz. catfish fillet
- 4 tablespoon panko breadcrumbs
- ¼ teaspoon dried oregano
- ¼ teaspoon ground ginger
- ¼ teaspoon ground thyme
- ¼ teaspoon salt
- ½ teaspoon ground paprika
- ½ teaspoon olive oil

Directions:

1. Cut the catfish fillet into 2 parts.
2. Put the panko breadcrumbs in the bowl.
3. Add dried oregano, ground ginger, ground thyme, salt, and ground paprika.
4. Stir the breadcrumb mixture gently.
5. Preheat the air fryer to 350 F.
6. Spray the air fryer basket tray with the olive oil inside.
7. Coat the catfish fillets in the breadcrumb mixture well.
8. Transfer the catfish fillets to the air fryer tray.
9. Cook the fish fillets for 10 minutes.
10. When the catfish fillets are cooked – transfer them to the serving plates.
11. Enjoy!

Nutrition: calories 296, fat 14.9, fiber 1, carbs 10.4, protein 28.4

Celery Chicken Wings

Prep time: 10 minutes
Cooking time: 28 minutes
Servings: 2
Ingredients

- 4 chicken wings
- 1 tablespoon cornstarch
- ¼ teaspoon salt
- ½ teaspoon garlic, sliced
- 1/3 teaspoon ground celery
- 1 oz fresh celery root, grated
- 1 tablespoon sour cream
- ¼ teaspoon cayenne pepper

Directions:

1. Rub the chicken wings with the sliced garlic, ground celery, grated celery root, sour cream, and cayenne pepper.
2. Mix up the meat and sprinkle the chicken wings with the salt.
3. Mix the meat again.
4. After this, sprinkle the chicken wings with the cornstarch. Shake the chicken wings well.
5. Preheat the air fryer to 400 F.
6. Place the chicken wings in the air fryer tray and cook for 25 minutes.
7. Then shake the chicken wings well and cook them for 3 minutes more.
8. Let the cooked chicken wings chill little.
9. Serve the meal!

Nutrition: calories 321, fat 12.5, fiber 0.4, carbs 5.6, protein 43.9

Rosemary Beef Steak

Prep time: 10 minutes
Cooking time: 20 minutes
Servings: 2
Ingredients

- 1 tablespoon fresh rosemary
- 2 beef steaks
- ½ teaspoon salt
- ½ teaspoon ground black pepper
- ¼ teaspoon cayenne pepper
- ¼ teaspoon turmeric
- 1 teaspoon olive oil
- ¼ teaspoon cilantro
- ½ teaspoon chili flakes
- 1 teaspoon onion powder

Directions:

1. Chop the fresh rosemary and combine it with the olive oil. Churn it.
2. Take the shallow bowl and combine salt, ground black pepper, cayenne pepper, turmeric, cilantro, chili flakes, and onion flakes together.
3. Shake the bowl well.
4. Then sprinkle the beef steak with the spices generously.
5. After this, rub every steak with the rosemary-oil mixture.
6. Preheat the air fryer to 400 F.
7. Put the beef steaks in the air fryer tray and cook for 10 minutes.
8. After this, flip the beef steaks to another side and cook the meat for 10 minutes more.
9. Transfer the cooked beef steak in the serving plates.
10. Enjoy!

Nutrition: calories 311, fat 12, fiber 1, carbs 2.7, protein 45.8

Creamy Cod Fillet

Prep time: 10 minutes
Cooking time: 14 minutes
Servings: 2
Ingredients

- 14 oz cod fillet
- 1 tablespoon Italian seasoning
- 3 tablespoon fresh spinach
- 1 teaspoon butter
- 1 teaspoon cream
- 1/3 teaspoon salt
- ¼ teaspoon turmeric
- ½ teaspoon onion powder
- 1 oz onion, diced

Directions:

1. Wash the spinach carefully and chop it.
2. Melt the butter and combine it with the cream. Churn it.
3. Combine the chopped spinach and cream mixture.
4. Rub the cod fillet with the salt, turmeric, and onion powder.
5. Then sprinkle the cod fillet with Italian seasoning well.
6. After this, combine the diced onion and spinach mixture. Stir it.
7. Put the spinach mixture on the cod fillet.
8. Then sew the cod fillet to make the tube or secure it with the toothpicks.
9. Preheat the air fryer to 355 F.
10. Cook the stuffed cod fillet for 14 minutes.
11. When the fish is cooked – slice it.
12. Enjoy!

Nutrition: calories 208, fat 5.9, fiber 0.5, carbs 2.9, protein 35.8

Butter Chicken Drumsticks

Prep time: 10 minutes
Cooking time: 25 minutes
Servings: 2
Ingredients

- 4 chicken drumsticks
- 1 teaspoon minced garlic
- ¼ teaspoon red pepper
- 1 tablespoon tomato sauce
- 1 teaspoon olive oil
- ½ teaspoon ground thyme
- ½ teaspoon paprika
- ½ teaspoon cayenne pepper
- ½ teaspoon mustard powder
- ½ teaspoon onion powder

Directions:

1. Take the big bowl and put the minced garlic, red pepper, tomato sauce, olive oil, ground thyme, paprika, cayenne pepper, mustard powder, and onion powder.
2. Stir the mixture with the help of the fork.
3. After this, rub the chicken drumsticks with the spice mixture.
4. Preheat the air fryer to 370 F.
5. Put the chicken drumsticks in the air fryer basket.
6. Cook the meal for 25 minutes.
7. Shake the chicken drumsticks during the cooking once.
8. Then transfer the chicken drumsticks to the serving plate.
9. Enjoy!

Nutrition: calories 194, fat 8.1, fiber 0.9, carbs 3.5, protein 26.1

Thyme Lamb Ribs

Prep time: 10 minutes
Cooking time: 30 minutes
Servings: 2
Ingredients

- 1 tablespoon flour
- 14 oz lamb ribs
- 1 egg
- 1 teaspoon thyme
- 1 teaspoon lemon juice
- 1 teaspoon cream
- 1 garlic clove, sliced
- 1 tablespoon canola oil
- 1 teaspoon rosemary
- ½ teaspoon paprika

Directions:

1. Sprinkle the lamb ribs with the thyme, lemon juice, cream, sliced garlic, canola oil, rosemary, and paprika.
2. Massage the lamb ribs gently.
3. Then crack the egg into the bowl and whisk it.
4. Dip the lamb ribs in the whisked egg.
5. After this, sprinkle the meat with the flour.
6. Preheat the air fryer to 345 F and put the lamb ribs in the air fryer basket.
7. Cook the meal for 25 minutes.
8. After this, increase the temperature to 370 F and cook the lamb ribs for 5 minutes more.
9. Let the cooked lamb ribs chill gently.
10. Enjoy!

Nutrition: calories 577, fat 36, fiber 0.8, carbs 4.8, protein 55.4

Curry Chicken Breast

Prep time: 20 minutes
Cooking time: 10 minutes
Servings: 2
Ingredients

- 15 oz chicken breast
- 1 tablespoon turmeric
- 1 teaspoon curry paste
- ½ yellow onion, diced
- 1 tablespoon mayonnaise
- ½ teaspoon onion powder
- ½ teaspoon garlic powder
- 1 teaspoon butter

Directions:

1. Combine together turmeric, curry paste, sided onion, mayonnaise, onion powder, and garlic powder.
2. Churn the mixture well.
3. Melt the butter and add churned mixture. Stir it.
4. After this, brush the chicken breast with the turmeric mixture and leave it for 10 minutes.
5. Preheat the air fryer to 380 F.
6. Put the chicken breast in the air fryer basket and cook for 10 minutes.
7. Flip the chicken breast into another side after 5 minutes of cooking.
8. Serve the cooked chicken breast immediately.
9. Enjoy!

Nutrition: calories 332, fat 11.5, fiber 1.4, carbs 8.2, protein 46.1

Maple Turkey Breast

Prep time: 10 minutes
Cooking time: 35 minutes
Servings: 2
Ingredients

- 1 teaspoon canola oil
- 1 teaspoon ground coriander
- ½ teaspoon turmeric
- ½ teaspoon onion powder
- ½ teaspoon oregano
- ½ teaspoon salt
- 1 teaspoon Dijon mustard
- 2 tablespoon maple syrup
- 1 tablespoon butter
- 14 oz turkey breast

Directions:

1. Combine the canola oil, ground coriander, turmeric, onion powder, oregano, and salt.
2. Churn the mixture to make the spice oil.
3. Brush the turkey breast with the spicy oil.
4. Melt the butter and combine it with the maple syrup, and Dijon mustard. Whisk it.
5. Preheat the air fryer to 360 F and put the turkey breast in the air fryer basket.
6. Cook the turkey breast for 25 minutes.
7. When the time is over – flip the turkey breast to another side.
8. Sprinkle the turkey breast with the maple syrup mixture generously.
9. Cook the meal for 10 minutes at 355 F.
10. Let the cooked turkey breast chill little. Slice it.
11. Enjoy!

Nutrition: calories 337, fat 4.5, fiber 1.4, carbs 23, protein 34.2

Rosemary Salmon Steak

Prep time: 10 minutes
Cooking time: 12 minutes
Servings: 2
Ingredients

- 2 salmon steaks
- ½ teaspoon salt
- ½ teaspoon ground coriander
- ½ teaspoon dried rosemary
- 1 teaspoon onion powder
- 1 tablespoon olive oil

Directions:

1. Sprinkle the salmon steaks with the salt, ground coriander, dried rosemary, and onion powder.
2. Then sprinkle the salmon steaks with the olive oil.
3. Put the salmon steaks in the air fryer basket and cook them for 12 minutes at 265 F.
4. When the salmon steaks are cooked - serve them immediately.
5. Enjoy!

Nutrition: calories 301, fat 18.1, fiber 0.2, carbs 1.2, protein 34.7

Stuffed Calamari

Prep time: 15 minutes
Cooking time: 10 minutes
Servings: 2
Ingredients:

- 2 calamari tubes
- 1 red sweet pepper
- 1 tablespoon fresh dill, chopped
- ½ teaspoon salt
- ½ teaspoon chili flakes
- ½ teaspoon turmeric
- 1 tablespoon olive oil
- 1 teaspoon garlic, sliced
- ½ teaspoon butter

Directions:

1. Preheat the air fryer to 400 F.
2. Put the red sweet pepper in the air fryer basket and cook it for 5 minutes.
3. Then remove the red sweet pepper from the air fryer basket tray and discard the seeds.
4. Chop the red sweet pepper and combine it with the chopped fresh dill.
5. Add sliced garlic and mix it.
6. After this, sprinkle the calamari tubes with the salt, chili flakes, turmeric, and olive oil.
7. Fill the calamari tubes with the red sweet pepper mixture and butter.
8. Secure the calamari tubes with the toothpicks.
9. Preheat the air fryer to 400 F.
10. Sprinkle the calamari tubes with the olive oil and put in the air fryer basket.
11. Cook the calamari tubes for 5 minutes.
12. When the meal is cooked – chill it little.
13. Serve it!

Nutrition: calories 192, fat 10, fiber 1.2, carbs 8.8, protein 16.1

Paprika Corn Beef

Prep time: 10 minutes
Cooking time: 14 minutes
Servings: 2
Ingredients

- 1 cup ground beef
- 1 white onion
- 5 tablespoon water
- ½ teaspoon ground black pepper
- ½ teaspoon salt
- ½ teaspoon ground paprika
- ½ teaspoon butter

Directions:

1. Preheat the air fryer to 400 F.
2. Pour water into the air fryer tray.
3. Peel the onion and slice it.
4. Add the sliced onion in the air fryer tray.
5. Put the tray in the air fryer and cook the onion for 4 minutes.
6. After this, remove the tray with the onion from the air fryer.
7. Add ground beef.
8. Sprinkle the ground beef with the ground black pepper, salt, ground paprika, and butter.
9. Stir the meat mixture carefully with the help of the fork.
10. Put the tray in the air fryer and cook the corned beef for 10 minutes at 400 F.
11. Then stir the ground beef mixture carefully and serve it.
12. Enjoy!

Nutrition: calories 280, fat 16.1, fiber 1.5, carbs 5.8, protein 27

Dijon Turkey Legs

Prep time: 10 minutes
Cooking time: 30 minutes
Servings: 2
Ingredients

- 2 turkey legs
- 2 tablespoon honey
- ½ teaspoon minced garlic
- 1 tablespoon Dijon mustard
- ¼ teaspoon ground coriander
- 1 teaspoon canola oil
- ½ teaspoon thyme
- ¼ teaspoon chili pepper

Directions:

1. Combine honey, minced garlic, Dijon mustard, ground coriander, canola oil, thyme, and chili pepper in the mixing bowl.
2. Churn the mixture well.
3. Brush the turkey legs with the sweet mixture generously.
4. Preheat the air fryer to 370 F.
5. Put the turkey legs in the air fryer basket and cook for 30 minutes.
6. Flip the turkey legs into another side after 15 minutes of cooking.
7. Then let the cooked turkey legs chill little.
8. Enjoy!

Nutrition: calories 239, fat 9.6, fiber 0.4, carbs 18.2, protein 20.3

Beef Zucchini Rings

Prep time: 15 minutes
Cooking time: 13 minutes
Servings: 2
Ingredients

- 1 zucchini
- 6 oz ground beef
- ½ teaspoon onion powder
- ½ teaspoon garlic powder
- ¼ teaspoon salt
- ½ teaspoon paprika
- 1 teaspoon olive oil

Directions:

1. Wash the zucchini carefully and cut it into the thick circles.
2. Then remove the flesh from the zucchini to make the zucchini rings.
3. Combine the ground beef, onion powder, garlic powder, salt, and paprika in the bowl.
4. Stir the meat with the help of the fork.
5. Then fill every zucchini ring with the meat mixture.
6. Sprinkle the zucchini rings with the olive oil.
7. Wrap every zucchini ring in the foil.
8. Preheat the air fryer to 360 F.
9. Put the zucchini rings in the air fryer basket and cook for 13 minutes.
10. When the meal is cooked – let it chill for 2-3 minutes.
11. Then discard the foil.
12. Serve and taste!

Nutrition: calories 200, fat 7.9, fiber 1.4, carbs 4.6, protein 27.3

Parmesan Peppers

Prep time: 20 minutes
Cooking time: 20 minutes
Servings: 2
Ingredients

- 2 sweet yellow peppers
- 1 garlic clove, sliced
- ½ white onion, diced
- ½ teaspoon salt
- 7 oz ground chicken
- 1 tablespoon tomato sauce
- ½ teaspoon ground black pepper
- 1 oz Parmesan, shredded
- 1 teaspoon butter
- ½ teaspoon olive oil

Directions:

1. Pour olive oil into the skillet and preheat it.
2. Then toss the diced onion in the olive oil and sauté it for 2-3 minutes on the medium heat. Stir it frequently.
3. Discard the seeds from the sweet yellow peppers.
4. Combine the sautéed onion with the sliced garlic, salt, ground chicken, tomato sauce, ground black pepper, and shredded Parmesan cheese.
5. Mix the ground chicken mixture.
6. Fill the sweet yellow peppers with the chicken mixture.
7. Preheat the air fryer to 400 F.
8. Put the butter over every stuffed pepper and transfer them to the air fryer.
9. Cook the stuffed peppers for 20 minutes.
10. When the meal is cooked – chill it gently and serve.

Nutrition: calories 328, fat 13.9, fiber 2.5, carbs 16.1, protein 35.7

Cabbage Beef Rolls

Prep time: 15 minutes
Cooking time: 20 minutes
Servings: 2
Ingredients

- 2 cabbage leaves
- 7 oz ground beef
- 1 egg white
- ¼ teaspoon salt
- ¼ teaspoon ground black pepper
- 1 tablespoon tomato sauce
- 1 teaspoon sour cream
- 1 teaspoon tomato juice
- ½ teaspoon olive oil
- 1 oz carrot, grated
- ½ onion, diced
- ¼ teaspoon thyme

Directions:

1. Whisk the egg white gently.
2. Combine the whisked egg white with the ground beef.
3. Sprinkle the meat mixture with salt, ground black pepper, grated carrot, diced onion, and thyme.
4. Stir the meat mixture with the help of the spoon carefully.
5. Separate the meat mixture into two parts.
6. Put the meat mixture on cabbage leaves.
7. Roll every cabbage leaf. Secure the cabbage leaves with the toothpicks if desired.
8. Preheat the air fryer to 360 F.
9. Put the cabbage rolls in the air fryer basket.
10. In the mixing bowl combine the tomato sauce, sour cream, and tomato juice.
11. Add olive oil and whisk it until homogenous.
12. Pour the tomato mixture over the cabbage rolls.
13. Cook the cabbage rolls for 20 minutes.
14. Flip the cabbage rolls into another side after 1- minutes of cooking.
15. When the cabbage rolls are cooked- let them chill gently.
16. Enjoy!

Nutrition: calories 231, fat 7.9, fiber 1.6, carbs 5.8, protein 32.7

Pork Bak

Prep time: 20 minutes
Cooking time: 50 minutes
Servings: 2
Ingredients

- 9 oz pork belly
- 3 cup water
- ½ teaspoon onion powder
- ½ teaspoon garlic powder
- ½ teaspoon ground black pepper
- ½ teaspoon cilantro
- ½ teaspoon ground ginger
- ¼ teaspoon ground cinnamon
- ½ teaspoon curry powder
- ½ teaspoon salt
- 1 teaspoon oregano
- 1 teaspoon olive oil
- 1 bay leaf
- 2 teaspoon lemon juice

Directions:

1. Pour water into the saucepan.
2. Put the pork belly and bay leaf in the water and close the lid.
3. Cook the pork belly for 20 minutes on the medium heat.
4. After this, remove the pork belly from the saucepan and dry it well.
5. Combine the onion powder, garlic powder, ground black pepper, cilantro, ground ginger, ground cinnamon, curry powder, salt, and oregano in the shallow bowl.
6. Stir the mixture.
7. Then rub the dried pork belly with the set of the spices well.
8. After this, combine the lemon juice and olive oil in the bowl and shake it gently.
9. Brush the pork belly with the oil-lemon mixture carefully.
10. Preheat the air fryer to 320 F.
11. Put the pork belly in the air fryer basket and cook it for 30 minutes more.
12. Turn the pork belly into another side after 15 minutes of cooking.
13. Slice the cooked pork belly and serve!
14. Enjoy!

Nutrition: calories 622, fat 36.9, fiber 1, carbs 2.8, protein 59.4

Chili Pork Slices

Prep time: 20 minutes
Cooking time: 25 minutes
Servings: 2
Ingredients

- 10 oz pork loin
- ½ carrot, peeled
- ¼ onion, peeled
- ¼ teaspoon salt
- ½ teaspoon red pepper
- ¼ teaspoon chili flakes
- ¼ teaspoon pesto sauce
- 2 teaspoon olive oil
- 1 teaspoon tomato juice
- ¼ teaspoon cayenne pepper

Directions:

1. Preheat an air fryer to 360 F.
2. Chop the carrot and onion into the small pieces.
3. Make as many cuts in the pork loin as you can.
4. Fill the pork loin cuts with the chopped carrot and onion.
5. Combine the olive oil with the salt, red pepper, chili flakes, pesto sauce, olive oil, tomato juice, and cayenne pepper.
6. Mix the mixture.
7. Brush the pork loin with the spicy mixture well and leave it for 10 minutes to marinate.
8. After this, transfer the pork loin in the air fryer basket.
9. Sprinkle the meat with the remaining spice mixture.
10. Cook the pork loin for 25 minutes.
11. Flip the pork loin into another side after 10 minutes of cooking.
12. When the time is over and the meat is cooked – remove it from the air fryer basket.
13. Slice it and serve.
14. Taste it!

Nutrition: calories 408, fat 24.8, fiber 1.1, carbs 5.3, protein 39.4

Onion Chicken Skin

Prep time: 15 minutes
Cooking time: 8 minutes
Servings: 2
Ingredients

- 1 onion, sautéed
- 4 oz chicken skin, 2 pieces
- 1 teaspoon butter
- ¼ teaspoon ground black pepper
- ½ teaspoon ground paprika
- ½ teaspoon oregano
- 2 oz Cheddar cheese, shredded
- ½ teaspoon turmeric
- ½ teaspoon olive oil
- 5 oz ground chicken
- ½ teaspoon sour cream

Directions:

1. Combine the ground chicken, turmeric, shredded cheese, sautéed onion, butter, ground black pepper, ground paprika, and oregano.
2. Mix the mixture up.
3. After this, add sour cream and mix it up again.
4. Put the ground chicken mixture on two pieces of the chicken skin.
5. Roll the chicken skin and sew it well.
6. After this, sprinkle the stuffed chicken skin with the olive oil.
7. Preheat the air fryer to 380 F.
8. Put the stuffed chicken skin in the air fryer basket and cook for 8 minutes.
9. The cooked chicken skin should have crunchy surface. Cook the chicken skin more if you don't get the desired doneness.
10. Let the meal chill little.
11. Enjoy!

Nutrition: calories 563, fat 41.2, fiber 1.7, carbs 6.6, protein 40

Oregano Pork Loaf

Prep time: 15 minutes
Cooking time: 15 minutes
Servings: 2
Ingredients

- 1 tablespoon tomato sauce
- 13 oz minced pork
- 1 egg
- 1 teaspoon dried oregano
- ½ teaspoon thyme
- ½ teaspoon salt
- ½ teaspoon turmeric
- ½ teaspoon onion powder
- ½ teaspoon garlic powder
- ¼ teaspoon cayenne pepper
- 1 teaspoon semolina
- 1 teaspoon butter

Directions:

1. Take the big mixing bowl and put there the minced pork, dried oregano, thyme, salt, turmeric, onion powder, garlic powder, cayenne pepper, and semolina.
2. Beat the egg in the minced pork mixture and mix it up.
3. Make the shape of the loaf from the minced pork mixture.
4. Preheat the air fryer to 370 F.
5. Melt the butter in the air fryer basket.
6. After this, put the pork loaf in the melted butter.
7. Cook the pork loaf for 15 minutes.
8. When the pork loaf is cooked – let it chill well.
9. Sprinkle the meatloaf with the tomato sauce.
10. After this, slice the pork loaf and serve.
11. Enjoy!

Nutrition: calories 330, fat 10.8, fiber 0.9, carbs 4, protein 51.7

Tender Beef Burgers

Prep time: 15 minutes
Cooking time: 17 minutes
Servings: 2
Ingredients

- ½ teaspoon lemon zest
- 13 oz ground beef
- 1/3 teaspoon ground black pepper
- ½ teaspoon salt
- ¼ teaspoon dried rosemary
- ½ teaspoon dried dill
- ½ teaspoon olive oil
- ¼ onion, diced
- ½ teaspoon minced garlic
- ¼ teaspoon cayenne pepper

Directions:

1. Preheat the air fryer to 370 F.
2. Put the ground beef in the bowl.
3. Sprinkle the ground beef with the lemon zest, ground black pepper, salt, dried rosemary, dried dill, diced onion, minced garlic, and cayenne pepper.
4. Mix the ground beef mixture with the help of the fingertips.
5. Make the medium burgers from the ground beef mixture.
6. Pour the olive oil into the air fryer basket.
7. Then put the beef burgers in the olive oil.
8. Cook the meal for 17 minutes. Do not stir the burgers during the cooking.
9. When the burgers are cooked – serve them immediately.
10. Enjoy!

Nutrition: calories 362, fat 12.7, fiber 0.6, carbs 2.2, protein 56.2

Honey Pork Meatballs

Prep time: 15 minutes
Cooking time: 16 minutes
Servings: 2
Ingredients

- 1 teaspoon honey
- 10 oz ground pork
- 1 teaspoon onion powder
- ¼ teaspoon butter
- ½ teaspoon dried cilantro
- ½ teaspoon oregano
- ¼ teaspoon salt
- 1 tablespoon tomato sauce
- ½ tablespoon flour
- ½ teaspoon olive oil
- ½ teaspoon ground ginger

Directions:

1. Put the ground pork in the bowl.
2. Sprinkle the meat with the onion powder, butter, dried cilantro, oregano, salt, flour, and ground ginger.
3. Mix the ground pork mixture carefully.
4. Preheat the air fryer to 360 F.
5. Sprinkle the air fryer basket with the olive oil.
6. Then make the small meatballs from the ground pork mixture.
7. Cook the meatballs in the olive oil for 10 minutes.
8. Meanwhile, combine the honey and tomato sauce.
9. Then brush the meatballs with the honey sauce.
10. Cook the meatballs for 6 minutes more.
11. Then let the meatballs chill gently.
12. Serve the meal!

Nutrition: calories 243, fat 6.7, fiber 0.5, carbs 6.3, protein 37.6

Cheddar Chicken Breast

Prep time: 15 minutes
Cooking time: 18 minutes
Servings: 2
Ingredients

- 1 ham slices
- 1/3 teaspoon ground black pepper
- 12 oz chicken breast, skinless, boneless
- 2 slices Cheddar cheese
- 1 teaspoon fresh parsley, chopped
- ¼ teaspoon salt
- ¼ teaspoon chili flakes
- 1 teaspoon salsa sauce
- ½ teaspoon olive oil

Directions:

1. Make the crosswise cut in the chicken breast.
2. Sprinkle the chicken breast with the ground black pepper, salt, chili flakes, and salsa sauce.
3. Massage the chicken breast gently.
4. Then put the ham slices and cheese slices in the chicken cut.
5. Secure the chicken breast with the toothpicks.
6. Then sprinkle the chicken breast with the olive oil.
7. Preheat the air fryer to 370 F.
8. Put the chicken breast in the air fryer basket and cook for 18 minutes.
9. When the chicken breast is cooked – pin it with the help of the knife. If the juice from the chicken is clear – it is cooked.
10. Serve the chicken breast hot.
11. Enjoy!

Nutrition: calories 341, fat 15.9, fiber 0.3, carbs 1.4, protein 45.5

Garlic Pork Satay

Prep time: 30 minutes
Cooking time: 14 minutes
Servings: 2
Ingredients

- 10 oz pork chops
- ½ teaspoon garlic clove, sliced
- ½ teaspoon chili paste
- 1 tablespoon soy sauce
- 1 teaspoon canola oil
- 2 oz shallot, chopped
- 4 teaspoon coconut milk

Directions:

1. Preheat the air fryer to 360 F.
2. Chop the pork chops into the satay pieces.
3. Place the pork satay pieces in the bowl.
4. Sprinkle the meat with the sliced garlic, chili paste, soy sauce, and chopped shallot.
5. Mix the meat mixture carefully with the help of the fingertips.
6. Leave the meat for 20 minutes to marinate.
7. Then sprinkle the air fryer basket with the olive oil.
8. Put the marinated meat in the air fryer and cook for 13 minutes.
9. Stir the meat 3 times during the cooking. The cooked meat should be golden brown.
10. Then sprinkle the meat with the coconut milk and cook it for 1 minute more.
11. Shake the meat and skewer it on the skewers.
12. Serve the pork satay hot.
13. Enjoy!

Nutrition: calories 621, fat 48.2, fiber 1.2, carbs 9.8, protein 37.4

Ginger Paprika Shrimps

Prep time: 15 minutes
Cooking time: 5 minutes
Servings: 2
Ingredients

- 4 tiger Royal shrimps
- ½ teaspoon ground ginger
- 1 teaspoon paprika
- 1 teaspoon olive oil
- ½ teaspoon garlic clove, minced
- ¼ teaspoon sriracha
- ½ teaspoon soy sauce
- ¼ teaspoon peanut butter

Directions:

1. Peel the shrimps.
2. Melt the peanut butter.
3. Combine the melted butter with the ground ginger, paprika, olive oil, minced garlic clove, sriracha, and soy sauce.
4. Churn the mixture well.
5. Then dip the shrimps in the peanut butter mixture.
6. Leave the shrimps for 10 minutes to marinate.
7. After this, preheat the air fryer to 400 F.
8. Put the shrimps in the air fryer basket and sprinkle with the remaining peanut butter sauce.
9. Cook the shrimps for 5 minutes.
10. After this, shake the shrimps well.
11. Serve the meal hot.
12. Enjoy!

Nutrition: calories 185, fat 4.8, fiber 0.5, carbs 1.5, protein 34.5

Tomato Beef

Prep time: 15 minutes
Cooking time: 25 minutes
Servings: 2
Ingredients

- 1 tomato
- 10 oz ground beef
- 1 teaspoon fresh thyme
- ½ teaspoon ground black pepper
- 1 tablespoon fresh parsley, chopped
- 1 teaspoon tomato sauce
- 1 teaspoon tomato juice
- ½ yellow onion, diced
- ¼ teaspoon ground bay leaf
- 1/3 teaspoon salt
- 1 teaspoon sour cream

Directions:

1. Wash the tomato and chop it.
2. Put the chopped tomato in the blender.
3. Add fresh thyme, chopped fresh parsley, ground black pepper, tomato sauce, tomato juice, salt, and sour cream.
4. Blend the mixture until smooth.
5. Sprinkle the smooth tomato mixture with the ground bay leaf and diced onion.
6. Then combine together the ground beef and tomato mixture. Mix it with the help of the spatula.
7. Preheat the air fryer to 360 F.
8. Put the ground beef mixture in the air fryer tray.
9. Cook the meal for 25 minutes.
10. Stir the ground beef after 10 minutes of cooking.
11. When the meal is cooked – stir it again.
12. Enjoy!

Nutrition: calories 289, fat 9.4, fiber 1.4, carbs 5, protein 43.9

Cayenne Lamb Steak

Prep time: 20 minutes
Cooking time: 30 minutes
Servings: 2
Ingredients

- 2 lamb steaks
- ½ teaspoon cayenne pepper
- ½ teaspoon ground black pepper
- ½ teaspoon salt
- ½ teaspoon lemon zest
- 1 tablespoon apple cider vinegar
- 1 teaspoon olive oil
- ½ teaspoon minced garlic
- ½ teaspoon dried rosemary

Directions:

1. Beat the lamb steak gently.
2. Combine the cayenne pepper, ground black pepper, salt, lemon zest, olive oil, minced garlic, and dried rosemary.
3. Churn the mixture well.
4. After this, sprinkle the lamb steaks with the apple cider vinegar.
5. Rub the lamb steaks with the olive oil mixture and leave for 10 minutes to marinate.
6. Preheat the air fryer to 330 F.
7. Put the lamb steaks in the air fryer basket.
8. Cook the lamb steaks for 15 minutes.
9. After this, flip the lamb steaks to another side and cook the meat for 15 minutes more.
10. When the lamb steaks are cooked – transfer them to the serving plates.
11. Enjoy!

Nutrition: calories 217, fat 9.5, fiber 0.4, carbs 1.2, protein 29.6

Rosemary Lamb Shank

Prep time: 20 minutes
Cooking time: 15 minutes
Servings: 2
Ingredients

- 15 oz lamb shank
- 1 teaspoon dried rosemary
- ½ teaspoon salt
- ¼ lime
- ½ teaspoon chili flakes
- 1 teaspoon apple cider vinegar
- 1 teaspoon canola oil
- ½ teaspoon ground ginger
- ½ teaspoon oregano

Directions:

1. Squeeze the juice from the lime.
2. Combine the lime juice with the dried rosemary, salt, chili flakes, apple cider vinegar, canola oil, ground ginger, and oregano.
3. Stir the spices gently.
4. Sprinkle the lamb shank with the spicy mixture and leave it for 15 minutes to let the meat soaks the spices.
5. Preheat the air fryer to 400 F.
6. Put the lamb shank in the air fryer basket.
7. Then sprinkle the lamb shank with the remaining spice mixture.
8. Cook the lamb shank for 15 minutes.
9. Shake the lamb shank after 8 minutes of cooking.
10. When the lamb shank is cooked – let it chill little.
11. Enjoy!

Nutrition: calories 425, fat 18.1, fiber 0.7, carbs 1.9, protein 59.9

Turmeric Chicken Necks

Prep time: 10 minutes
Cooking time: 15 minutes
Servings: 2
Ingredients

- 9 oz chicken necks
- ½ teaspoon salt
- 1 teaspoon turmeric
- 1 tablespoon sour cream
- ½ teaspoon garlic sauce
- 1 teaspoon olive oil
- ½ teaspoon ground paprika

Directions:

1. Put the chicken necks in the bowl.
2. Sprinkle the chicken necks with the salt, turmeric, sour cream, garlic sauce, ground paprika, and olive oil.
3. Mix the chicken necks with the help of the fingertips.
4. Preheat the air fryer to 370 F.
5. Put the chicken necks in the air fryer basket.
6. Cook the chicken necks for 15 minutes.
7. Shake the chicken necks twice during the cooking.
8. When the meal is cooked – shake it one more time.
9. Transfer the cooked chicken necks in the serving plates.
10. Enjoy!

Nutrition: calories 353, fat 26.9, fiber 0.4, carbs 1.3, protein 25.4

Yogurt Chicken Kebab

Prep time: 15 minutes
Cooking time: 10 minutes
Servings: 2
Ingredients

- 12 oz chicken fillet
- 1 teaspoon curry powder
- ½ teaspoon garlic powder
- ½ teaspoon onion powder
- 2 tablespoon Plain yogurt
- ½ teaspoon salt
- ½ teaspoon ground paprika
- ¼ teaspoon chili flakes

Directions:

1. Cut the chicken fillet into the cubes.
2. Combine Plain yogurt with the curry powder, garlic powder, onion powder, salt, chili flakes, and ground paprika.
3. Whisk it carefully.
4. Then dip the chicken cubes in the yogurt mixture.
5. Preheat the air fryer to 360 F.
6. Put the chicken cubes in the air fryer basket.
7. Cook the chicken kebabs for 10 minutes.
8. When the time is over – shake the chicken kebabs gently.
9. Transfer the meal to the serving plates.
10. Enjoy!

Nutrition: calories 343, fat 13, fiber 0.6, carbs 3, protein 50.5

Dijon Chicken

Prep time: 10 minutes
Cooking time: 12 minutes
Servings: 2
Ingredients

- 12 oz chicken breast, skinless, boneless, chopped
- 2 teaspoon curry paste
- 1 teaspoon Dijon mustard
- 1 teaspoon minced garlic
- 1 yellow onion, sliced
- ½ teaspoon olive oil
- ¼ cup milk
- ¼ cup chicken stock

Directions:

1. Preheat the air fryer to 380 F.
2. Put the chopped chicken in the air fryer basket.
3. Then add the sliced onion.
4. After this, sprinkle the chicken with the Dijon mustard, minced garlic, olive oil, and milk.
5. Combine the curry paste and chicken stock in the bowl and whisk it.
6. When the curry paste is dissolved – pour the liquid into the air fryer basket.
7. Stir the chicken gently using the wooden spatula.
8. Cook the curry chicken for 12 minutes.
9. After this, stir the curry chicken gently and serve it.
10. Enjoy!

Nutrition: calories 280, fat 9.2, fiber 1.3, carbs 8.7, protein 38.2

Pork Ribs

Prep time: 15 minutes
Cooking time: 12 minutes
Servings: 2
Ingredients:

- 13 oz pork ribs
- 1 teaspoon cornstarch
- 1 teaspoon soy sauce
- 1 teaspoon honey
- ½ teaspoon tomato sauce
- ½ teaspoon garlic, sliced
- 1 teaspoon olive oil
- 1 teaspoon apple cider vinegar
- ½ teaspoon butter
- ½ teaspoon dried rosemary
- ½ teaspoon ground ginger

Directions:

1. Put the pork ribs in the bowl.
2. Sprinkle the pork ribs with the soy sauce, honey, tomato sauce, sliced garlic, olive oil, apple cider vinegar, dried rosemary, and ground ginger.
3. Mix the pork ribs gently.
4. After this, preheat the air fryer to 400 F.
5. Sprinkle the pork ribs with the cornstarch and shake them.
6. Toss the butter in the air fryer basket.
7. Melt the butter and add the pork ribs.
8. Cook the pork ribs for 12 minutes.
9. Shake the pork ribs in 5 minutes.
10. When the pork ribs are cooked – they will be a little bit crunchy.
11. Transfer the meal to the serving plates.
12. Enjoy!

Nutrition: calories 347, fat 4.7, fiber 4.5, carbs 45.3, protein 35.1

Coconut Chili Beef Strips

Prep time: 20 minutes
Cooking time: 16 minutes
Servings: 2
Ingredients:

- 1 teaspoon chili pepper
- ¼ teaspoon sriracha
- 2 teaspoon coconut milk
- 1 teaspoon peanut butter
- 1 teaspoon butter
- ½ teaspoon dried rosemary
- 14 oz beef tenderloin
- ½ teaspoon sage

Directions:

1. Cut the beef tenderloin into the strips.
2. Put the beef strips in the bowl.
3. Sprinkle the beef strips with the chili pepper, sriracha, coconut milk, peanut butter, butter, dried rosemary, and sage.
4. Mix the beef strips with the help of the fingertips.
5. After this, leave the beef strips for 10 minutes in the fridge to marinate.
6. Preheat the air fryer to 400 F.
7. Put the beef strips in the air fryer basket.
8. Cook the beef strips for 10 minutes.
9. The shake the beef strips and cook for 6 minutes more.
10. When the beef strips are cooked – chill them till the room temperature.
11. Enjoy!

Nutrition: calories 456, fat 22.7, fiber 0.6, carbs 1.5, protein 58.3

Oat Chicken Sausages

Prep time: 25 minutes
Cooking time: 10 minutes
Servings: 2
Ingredients:

- 10 oz ground chicken
- ½ teaspoon garlic powder
- 1 teaspoon onion, grated
- ½ teaspoon salt
- 1 teaspoon butter
- ½ teaspoon dried dill
- 1 egg white
- 1 teaspoon sour cream
- 1 teaspoon oatmeal
- ¼ teaspoon canola oil

Directions:

1. Whisk the egg white and pour it into the bowl.
2. Add ground chicken, garlic powder, grated onion, salt, and dried dill.
3. Then add oatmeal.
4. Melt the butter and add it to the ground chicken.
5. Add sour cream and mix the chicken mixture.
6. Then form the medium sausages and place them in them in the freezer for 10 minutes.
7. Preheat the air fryer to 400 F.
8. Sprinkle the frozen chicken sausages with the canola oil and place them in the air fryer basket.
9. Cook the chicken sausages for 5 minutes on each side.
10. When the sausages are cooked – serve them hot.
11. Enjoy!

Nutrition: calories 311, fat 13.5, fiber 0.2, carbs 1.6, protein 43.2

Side Dishes

Parmesan Sweet Potato Casserole

Prep time: 15 minutes
Cooking time: 35 minutes
Servings: 2
Ingredients:

- 2 sweet potatoes, peeled
- ½ yellow onion, sliced
- ½ cup cream
- ¼ cup spinach
- 2 oz Parmesan cheese, shredded
- ½ teaspoon salt
- 1 tomato
- 1 teaspoon olive oil

Directions:

1. Chop the sweet potatoes.
2. Chop the tomato.
3. Chop the spinach.
4. Spray the air fryer tray with the olive oil.
5. Then place on the layer of the chopped sweet potato.
6. Add the layer of the sliced onion.
7. After this, sprinkle the sliced onion with the chopped spinach and tomatoes.
8. Sprinkle the casserole with the salt and shredded cheese.
9. Pour cream.
10. Preheat the air fryer to 390 F.
11. Cover the air fryer tray with the foil.
12. Cook the casserole for 35 minutes.
13. When the casserole is cooked – serve it.
14. Enjoy!

Nutrition: calories 93, fat 1.8, fiber 3.4, carbs 20.3, protein 1.8

Spicy Zucchini Slices

Prep time: 10 minutes
Cooking time: 6 minutes
Servings: 2
Ingredients:

- 1 teaspoon cornstarch
- 1 zucchini
- ½ teaspoon chili flakes
- 1 tablespoon flour
- 1 egg
- ¼ teaspoon salt

Directions:

1. Slice the zucchini and sprinkle with the chili flakes and salt.
2. Crack the egg into the bowl and whisk it.
3. Dip the zucchini slices in the whisked egg.
4. Combine together cornstarch with the flour. Stir it.
5. Coat the zucchini slices with the cornstarch mixture.
6. Preheat the air fryer to 400 F.
7. Place the zucchini slices in the air fryer tray.
8. Cook the zucchini slices for 4 minutes.
9. After this, flip the slices to another side and cook for 2 minutes more.
10. Serve the zucchini slices hot.
11. Enjoy!

Nutrition: calories 67, fat 2.4, fiber 1.2, carbs 7.7, protein 4.4

Cheddar Potato Gratin

Prep time: 15 minutes
Cooking time: 20 minutes
Servings: 2
Ingredients:

- 2 potatoes
- 1/3 cup half and half
- 1 tablespoon oatmeal flour
- ¼ teaspoon ground black pepper
- 1 egg
- 2 oz Cheddar cheese

Directions:

1. Wash the potatoes and slice them into thin pieces.
2. Preheat the air fryer to 365 F.
3. Put the potato slices in the air fryer and cook them for 10 minutes.
4. Meanwhile, combine the half and half, oatmeal flour, and ground black pepper.
5. Crack the egg into the liquid and whisk it carefully.
6. Shred Cheddar cheese.
7. When the potato is cooked – take 2 ramekins and place the potatoes on them.
8. Pour the half and half mixture.
9. Sprinkle the gratin with shredded Cheddar cheese.
10. Cook the gratin for 10 minutes at 360 F.
11. Serve the meal immediately.
12. Enjoy!

Nutrition: calories 353, fat 16.6, fiber 5.4, carbs 37.2, protein 15

Salty Lemon Artichokes

Prep time: 15 minutes
Cooking time: 45 minutes
Servings: 2
Ingredients:

- 1 lemon
- 2 artichokes
- 1 teaspoon kosher salt
- 1 garlic head
- 2 teaspoon olive oil

Directions:

1. Cut off the edges of the artichokes.
2. Cut the lemon into the halves.
3. Peel the garlic head and chop the garlic cloves roughly.
4. Then place the chopped garlic in the artichokes.
5. Sprinkle the artichokes with the olive oil and kosher salt.
6. Then squeeze the lemon juice into the artichokes.
7. Wrap the artichokes in the foil.
8. Preheat the air fryer to 330 F.
9. Place the wrapped artichokes in the air fryer and cook for 45 minutes.
10. When the artichokes are cooked – discard the foil and serve.
11. Enjoy!

Nutrition: calories 133, fat 5, fiber 9.7, carbs 21.7, protein 6

Asparagus & Parmesan

Prep time: 10 minutes
Cooking time: 6 minutes
Servings: 2
Ingredients:

- 1 teaspoon sesame oil
- 11 oz asparagus
- 1 teaspoon chicken stock
- ½ teaspoon ground white pepper
- 3 oz Parmesan

Directions:

1. Wash the asparagus and chop it roughly.
2. Sprinkle the chopped asparagus with the chicken stock and ground white pepper.
3. Then sprinkle the vegetables with the sesame oil and shake them.
4. Place the asparagus in the air fryer basket.
5. Cook the vegetables for 4 minutes at 400 F.
6. Meanwhile, shred Parmesan cheese.
7. When the time is over – shake the asparagus gently and sprinkle with the shredded cheese.
8. Cook the asparagus for 2 minutes more at 400 F.
9. After this, transfer the cooked asparagus in the serving plates.
10. Serve and taste it!

Nutrition: calories 189, fat 11.6, fiber 3.4, carbs 7.9, protein 17.2

Carrot Lentil Burgers

Prep time: 10 minutes
Cooking time: 12 minutes
Servings: 2
Ingredients:

- 6 oz lentils, cooked
- 1 egg
- 2 oz carrot, grated
- 1 teaspoon semolina
- ½ teaspoon salt
- 1 teaspoon turmeric
- 1 tablespoon butter

Directions:

1. Crack the egg into the bowl and whisk it.
2. Add the cooked lentils and mash the mixture with the help of the fork.
3. Then sprinkle the mixture with the grated carrot, semolina, salt, and turmeric.
4. Mix it up and make the medium burgers.
5. Put the butter into the lentil burgers. It will make them juicy.
6. Preheat the air fryer to 360 F.
7. Put the lentil burgers in the air fryer and cook for 12 minutes.
8. Flip the burgers into another side after 6 minutes of cooking.
9. Then chill the cooked lentil burgers and serve them.
10. Enjoy!

Nutrition: calories 404, fat 9, fiber 26.9, carbs 56, protein 25.3

Corn on Cobs

Prep time: 10 minutes
Cooking time: 10 minutes
Servings: 2
Ingredients:

- 2 fresh corn on cobs
- 2 teaspoon butter
- 1 teaspoon salt
- 1 teaspoon paprika
- ¼ teaspoon olive oil

Directions:

1. Preheat the air fryer to 400 F.
2. Rub the corn on cobs with the salt and paprika.
3. Then sprinkle the corn on cobs with the olive oil.
4. Place the corn on cobs in the air fryer basket.
5. Cook the corn on cobs for 10 minutes.
6. When the time is over – transfer the corn on cobs in the serving plates and rub with the butter gently.
7. Serve the meal immediately.
8. Enjoy!

Nutrition: calories 122, fat 5.5, fiber 2.4, carbs 17.6, protein 3.2

Sugary Carrot Strips

Prep time: 10 minutes
Cooking time: 10 minutes
Servings: 2
Ingredients:

- 2 carrots
- 1 teaspoon brown sugar
- 1 teaspoon olive oil
- 1 tablespoon soy sauce
- 1 teaspoon honey
- ½ teaspoon ground black pepper

Directions:

1. Peel the carrot and cut it into the strips.
2. Then put the carrot strips in the bowl.
3. Sprinkle the carrot strips with the olive oil, soy sauce, honey, and ground black pepper.
4. Shake the mixture gently.
5. Preheat the air fryer to 360 F.
6. Cook the carrot for 10 minutes.
7. After this, shake the carrot strips well.
8. Enjoy!

Nutrition: calories 67, fat 2.4, fiber 1.7, carbs 11.3, protein 1.1

Onion Green Beans

Prep time: 10 minutes
Cooking time: 12 minutes
Servings: 2
Ingredients:

- 11 oz green beans
- 1 tablespoon onion powder
- 1 tablespoon olive oil
- ½ teaspoon salt
- ¼ teaspoon chili flakes

Directions:

1. Wash the green beans carefully and place them in the bowl.
2. Sprinkle the green beans with the onion powder, salt, chili flakes, and olive oil.
3. Shake the green beans carefully.
4. Preheat the air fryer to 400 F.
5. Put the green beans in the air fryer and cook for 8 minutes.
6. After this, shake the green beans and cook them for 4 minutes more at 400 F.
7. When the time is over – shake the green beans.
8. Serve the side dish and enjoy!

Nutrition: calories 1205, fat 7.2, fiber 5.5, carbs 13.9, protein 3.2

Mozzarella Radish Salad

Prep time: 10 minutes
Cooking time: 20 minutes
Servings: 2
Ingredients:

- 8 oz radish
- 4 oz Mozzarella
- 1 teaspoon balsamic vinegar
- ½ teaspoon salt
- 1 tablespoon olive oil
- 1 teaspoon dried oregano

Directions:

1. Wash the radish carefully and cut it into the halves.
2. Preheat the air fryer to 360 F.
3. Put the radish halves in the air fryer basket.
4. Sprinkle the radish with the salt and olive oil.
5. Cook the radish for 20 minutes.
6. Shake the radish after 10 minutes of cooking.
7. When the time is over – transfer the radish to the serving plate.
8. Chop Mozzarella roughly.
9. Sprinkle the radish with Mozzarella, balsamic vinegar, and dried oregano.
10. Stir it gently with the help of 2 forks.
11. Serve it immediately.

Nutrition: calories 241, fat 17.2, fiber 2.1, carbs 6.4, protein 16.9

Cremini Mushroom Satay

Prep time: 10 minutes
Cooking time: 6 minutes
Servings: 2
Ingredients:

- 7 oz cremini mushrooms
- 2 tablespoon coconut milk
- 1 tablespoon butter
- 1 teaspoon chili flakes
- ½ teaspoon balsamic vinegar
- ½ teaspoon curry powder
- ½ teaspoon white pepper

Directions:

1. Wash the mushrooms carefully.
2. Then sprinkle the mushrooms with the chili flakes, curry powder, and white pepper.
3. Preheat the air fryer to 400 F.
4. Toss the butter in the air fryer basket and melt it.
5. Put the mushrooms in the air fryer and cook for 2 minutes.
6. Shake the mushrooms well and sprinkle with the coconut milk and balsamic vinegar.
7. Cook the mushrooms for 4 minutes more at 400 F.
8. Then skewer the mushrooms on the wooden sticks and serve.
9. Enjoy!

Nutrition: calories 116, fat 9.5, fiber 1.3, carbs 5.6, protein 3

Eggplant Ratatouille

Prep time: 15 minutes
Cooking time: 15 minutes
Servings: 2
Ingredients:

- 1 eggplant
- 1 sweet yellow pepper
- 3 cherry tomatoes
- 1/3 white onion, chopped
- ½ teaspoon garlic clove, sliced
- 1 teaspoon olive oil
- ½ teaspoon ground black pepper
- ½ teaspoon Italian seasoning

Directions:

1. Preheat the air fryer to 360 F.
2. Peel the eggplants and chop them.
3. Put the chopped eggplants in the air fryer basket.
4. Chop the cherry tomatoes and add them to the air fryer basket.
5. Then add chopped onion, sliced garlic clove, olive oil, ground black pepper, and Italian seasoning.
6. Chop the sweet yellow pepper roughly and add it to the air fryer basket.
7. Shake the vegetables gently and cook for 15 minutes.
8. Stir the meal after 8 minutes of cooking.
9. Transfer the cooked ratatouille in the serving plates.
10. Enjoy!

Nutrition: calories 149, fat 3.7, fiber 11.7, carbs 28.9, protein 5.1

Cheddar Portobello Mushrooms

Prep time: 15 minutes
Cooking time: 6 minutes
Servings: 2
Ingredients:

- 2 Portobello mushroom hats
- 2 slices Cheddar cheese
- ¼ cup panko breadcrumbs
- ½ teaspoon salt
- ½ teaspoon ground black pepper
- 1 egg
- 1 teaspoon oatmeal
- 2 oz bacon, chopped cooked

Directions:

1. Crack the egg into the bowl and whisk it.
2. Combine the ground black pepper, oatmeal, salt, and breadcrumbs in the separate bowl.
3. Dip the mushroom hats in the whisked egg.
4. After this, coat the mushroom hats in the breadcrumb mixture.
5. Preheat the air fryer to 400 F.
6. Place the mushrooms in the air fryer basket tray and cook for 3 minutes.
7. After this, put the chopped bacon and sliced cheese over the mushroom hats and cook the meal for 3 minutes.
8. When the meal is cooked – let it chill gently.
9. Enjoy!

Nutrition: calories 376, fat 24.1, fiber 1.8, carbs 14.6, protein 25.2

Creamy Cauliflower Head

Prep time: 10 minutes
Cooking time: 17 minutes
Servings: 2
Ingredients:

- 12 oz cauliflower head
- 2 tablespoon cream
- 1 tablespoon flour
- ½ teaspoon ground black pepper
- 1 teaspoon turmeric
- 1 teaspoon salt
- 1 teaspoon olive oil

Directions:

1. Wash the cauliflower head carefully.
2. Combine the cream and flour in the bowl.
3. Add ground black pepper and turmeric.
4. Whisk the mixture.
5. Then sprinkle the cauliflower head with the cream mixture. Let the cauliflower soaks the cream.
6. Sprinkle the cauliflower with salt.
7. Preheat the air fryer to 360 F.
8. Put the cauliflower r head in the air fryer tray.
9. Cook the vegetables for 12 minutes.
10. After this, sprinkle the cauliflower with the olive oil.
11. Cook the cauliflower head for 5 minutes at 390 F.
12. When the cauliflower is cooked – it will have the light brown crusted surface.
13. Serve it and enjoy!

Nutrition: calories 90, fat 3.3, fiber 4.7, carbs 13.4, protein 4

Cream Cheese Baked Potato

Prep time: 15 minutes
Cooking time: 22 minutes
Servings: 2
Ingredients:

- 1 teaspoon cream cheese
- 2 potatoes
- ½ teaspoon salt
- ½ teaspoon white pepper
- ½ onion, sautéed
- 1 oz sweet peas, cooked
- 1 teaspoon butter
- ½ teaspoon minced garlic

Directions:

1. Preheat the air fryer to 365 F.
2. Wash the potatoes carefully and place them in the air fryer basket.
3. Cook the potatoes for 18 minutes.
4. Meanwhile, churn together the cream cheese, minced garlic, and white pepper.
5. Add the sautéed onion and sweet peas.
6. Add salt and mix the mixture up.
7. After this, melt the butter.
8. When the time is over – remove the baked potatoes from the air fryer and cut them into the halves.
9. Scoop the flesh from the potatoes gently.
10. Combine the potato flesh and cream cheese mixture together.
11. Then fill the potato halves with the cream cheese mixture.
12. Put the potatoes in the air fryer.
13. Cook the meal for 4 minutes at 400 F.
14. When the potatoes are cooked – let them chill gently.
15. Enjoy!

Nutrition: calories 195, fat 2.8, fiber 6.6, carbs 38.7, protein 4.9

Cayenne Pepper Brussels Sprouts

Prep time: 10 minutes
Cooking time: 15 minutes
Servings: 2
Ingredients:

- 1 tablespoon butter
- 10 oz Brussel sprouts
- ½ teaspoon cayenne pepper
- 4 tablespoon chicken stock
- 1 teaspoon paprika
- ½ teaspoon lemon juice
- ¼ teaspoon salt

Directions:

1. Cut Brussel sprouts into the halves.
2. Churn the butter with the cayenne pepper and paprika.
3. Add salt and stir it carefully.
4. Then sprinkle Brussels sprouts halves with the lemon juice.
5. Preheat the air fryer to 380 F.
6. Put the butter mixture in the air fryer basket.
7. Melt the butter and add Brussel sprouts halves.
8. Cook the vegetables for 15 minutes. Shake the vegetables after 7 minutes of cooking.
9. Then let the cooked vegetables chill gently.
10. Enjoy!

Nutrition: calories 118, fat 6.5, fiber 5.8, carbs 13.9, protein 5.2

Bell Pepper Slices

Prep time: 20 minutes
Cooking time: 10 minutes
Servings: 2
Ingredients:

- 1 sweet red pepper
- 1 yellow sweet pepper
- 1 garlic clove
- 1 tablespoon apple cider vinegar
- 1 teaspoon olive oil
- ½ teaspoon dried dill
- ½ teaspoon dried parsley
- 1 teaspoon butter
- 1 pinch salt

Directions:

1. Wash the sweet peppers carefully and discard seeds.
2. Slice the sweet peppers.
3. Preheat the air fryer to 400 F.
4. Toss the butter in the air fryer basket and melt it.
5. Then add the sweet peppers slices.
6. Cook the sweet peppers for 10 minutes.
7. Shake them well after 5 minutes of cooking.
8. Meanwhile, peel the garlic clove and slice it.
9. Combine the sliced garlic with the apple cider vinegar and olive oil.
10. Add dried dill and dried parsley.
11. Sprinkle the mixture with the pinch of salt and whisk it well.
12. When the peppers are cooked – let the chill till the room temperature.
13. Then sprinkle the sweet peppers with the oily mixture well.
14. Put the meal in the fridge for 10 minutes.
15. Serve it!

Nutrition: calories 86, fat 4.6, fiber 1.7, carbs 11.1, protein 1.7

Sugary Pumpkin Wedges

Prep time: 15 minutes
Cooking time: 8 minutes
Servings: 2
Ingredients:

- 1 teaspoon raisins
- 12 oz pumpkin
- 1 teaspoon ground cinnamon
- 1 teaspoon butter
- 5 tablespoon water
- 2 tablespoon brown sugar
- 1 teaspoon fresh ginger, grated

Directions:

1. Peel the pumpkin and cut it into the serving wedges.
2. Melt the butter and combine it together with the ground cinnamon, brown sugar, and grated ginger.
3. Churn the mixture gently.
4. Rub every pumpkin wedge with the butter mixture well. Leave it.
5. Preheat the air fryer to 390 F.
6. Pour water into the air fryer basket.
7. Add raisins and pumpkin wedges.
8. After this, add all the remaining juice from the pumpkin wedges.
9. Cook the pumpkin for 5 minutes.
10. After this, flip the pumpkin wedges into another side.
11. Cook the pumpkin wedges for 3 minutes more.
12. Then transfer the cooked pumpkin wedges into the serving plates.
13. Sprinkle the pumpkin wedges with the raisins.
14. Enjoy!

Nutrition: calories 119, fat 2.5, fiber 5.7, carbs 25.4, protein 2.1

Cream Cheese Spinach

Prep time: 15 minutes
Cooking time: 10 minutes
Servings: 2
Ingredients:

- ¼ cup cream
- 1 tablespoon cream cheese
- 1 cup spinach
- ½ onion, diced, boiled
- ½ teaspoon salt
- 1 teaspoon butter
- ½ teaspoon ground black pepper
- 2 bacon slices, cooked, chopped
- ½ teaspoon paprika

Directions:

1. Preheat the air fryer to 330 F.
2. Toss the butter in the air fryer basket and melt.
3. Meanwhile, chop the spinach and sprinkle it with the salt.
4. Let the spinach gives the juice.
5. When the butter is melted – put the spinach with the remaining juice in the air fryer basket.
6. Sprinkle the spinach with the cream cheese, cream, diced onion, ground black pepper, and paprika.
7. Stir the mixture gently with the help of the wooden spatula.
8. Cook the spinach for 5 minutes.
9. After this, stir the spinach gently and add chopped bacon.
10. Cook the spinach for 5 minutes more.
11. Then stir the cooked meal carefully.
12. Transfer the cooked spinach to the serving plates.
13. Serve it!

Nutrition: calories 174, fat 13.4, fiber 1.3, carbs 5.1, protein 8.6

Creamy Leek

Prep time: 10 minutes
Cooking time: 11 minutes
Servings: 2
Ingredients:

- ½ teaspoon baking soda
- 1 tablespoon sugar
- 11 oz leek
- 3 tablespoon cream
- ¼ teaspoon salt
- 1 tablespoon butter
- 3 tablespoon chicken stock
- ¼ teaspoon turmeric

Directions:

1. Chop the leek.
2. Preheat the air fryer to 390 F.
3. Toss the butter there and melt it.
4. Then add cream and chicken stock.
5. After this, add the chopped leek.
6. Sprinkle the leek with the sugar, salt, baking soda, and turmeric.
7. Stir it carefully.
8. Cook the leek for 5 minutes.
9. After this, shake the leek carefully and cook for 6 minutes more.
10. When the leek is soft and light brown – it is cooked.
11. Let it chill for 3 minutes.
12. Serve the meal.

Nutrition: calories 182, fat 7.3, fiber 2.9, carbs 28.9, protein 2.6

Paprika Hasselback Potatoes

Prep time: 15 minutes
Cooking time: 30 minutes
Servings: 2
Ingredients:

- 2 medium potatoes
- 4 bacon slices
- ½ teaspoon salt
- ½ teaspoon ground black pepper
- ½ teaspoon ground paprika
- 1 teaspoon olive oil
- ½ teaspoon thyme
- ¼ teaspoon sage

Directions:

1. Wash the potatoes carefully but do not peel them.
2. Cut the slits in the potatoes to not cut them completely.
3. Place the sliced bacon into the potato slits.
4. Then sprinkle every Hasselback potato with the salt, ground black pepper, ground paprika, olive oil, thyme, and sage.
5. Preheat the air fryer to 400 F.
6. Put the Hasselback potatoes in the air fryer basket.
7. Cook the Hasselback potatoes for 30 minutes.
8. When the meal is cooked – chill it till the room temperature.
9. Serve it!

Nutrition: calories 376, fat 18.5, fiber 5.6, carbs 34.9, protein 17.8

Marinated Eggplants with Sesame Seeds

Prep time: 20 minutes
Cooking time: 12 minutes
Servings: 2
Ingredients:

- 2 eggplants
- 1 tablespoon sesame seeds
- 1 teaspoon canola oil
- 1 teaspoon apple cider vinegar
- ½ teaspoon chili flakes
- ¼ cup chicken stock
- 1 pinch salt
- ½ teaspoon lemon juice

Directions:

1. Peel the eggplants and cut them into the medium cubes.
2. Preheat the air fryer to 390 F.
3. Put the eggplants in the air fryer basket and sprinkle with the chicken stock salt.
4. Cook the eggplants for 8 minutes.
5. Shake the eggplants after 4 minutes of cooking.
6. Then drain the eggplants and transfer them to the bowl.
7. Sprinkle the vegetables with the sesame seeds, apple cider vinegar, chili flakes, salt, and lemon juice.
8. Mix the vegetables gently and put them in the fridge for at least 10 minutes to marinate.
9. Serve the cooked meal cold.
10. Enjoy!

Nutrition: calories 186, fat 5.6, fiber 19.9, carbs 33.4, protein 6.3

Cheddar Mac'n'Cheese

Prep time: 15 minutes
Cooking time: 5 minutes
Servings: 2
Ingredients:

- 6 oz mac, boiled
- 3 oz Cheddar cheese, shredded
- 2 oz Parmesan, shredded
- 1/3 cup half and half
- 1 teaspoon butter
- ½ teaspoon salt
- ½ teaspoon dried oregano

Directions:

1. Toss the butter in the saucepan and melt it.
2. Add half and half.
3. Then sprinkle the liquid with the shredded Parmesan and Cheddar cheese.
4. Add salt and dried oregano.
5. Stir the mixture and simmer it on the medium heat for 3 minutes or till the cheese is melted and liquid is homogenous.
6. Preheat the air fryer to 360 F.
7. Put the cooked mac in the air fryer basket.
8. Add the melted cheese mixture and stir.
9. Cook the mac for 5 minutes.
10. When the mac is cooked – it will have the light brown crust.
11. Serve the meal immediately.
12. Enjoy!

Nutrition: calories 578, fat 28.7, fiber 0.2, carbs 50.1, protein 30.6

White Oregano Cabbage

Prep time: 10 minutes
Cooking time: 7 minutes
Servings: 2
Ingredients:

- 12 oz white cabbage
- 1 tablespoon onion powder
- 1 teaspoon peanut butter
- ½ teaspoon olive oil
- 1 teaspoon oregano
- ½ tablespoon dried dill
- ¼ teaspoon ground black pepper

Directions:

1. Slice the cabbage into the thick wedges.
2. Rub the cabbage with the onion powder, oregano, dried dill, and ground black pepper.
3. Then sprinkle the cabbage wedges with the olive oil.
4. Massage every cabbage wedge gently from each side.
5. Preheat the air fryer to 360 F.
6. Put the cabbage wedges in the air fryer basket.
7. Add the peanut butter and cook the meal for 4 minutes.
8. After this, flip the cabbage wedges to another side and cook for 3 minutes.
9. Then transfer the cooked meal to the serving plates.
10. Enjoy!

Nutrition: calories 85, fat 2.8, fiber 5.1, carbs 14.3, protein 3.5

Creamy Broccoli Florets

Prep time: 15 minutes
Cooking time: 6 minutes
Servings: 2
Ingredients:

- 1 egg
- ¼ cup cream
- ½ teaspoon salt
- 2 tablespoon flour
- 1 teaspoon olive oil
- 12 oz broccoli

Directions:

1. Wash the broccoli and separate it into the medium florets.
2. Crack the egg into the bowl and whisk it.
3. Combine the egg with the cream and salt.
4. Stir the mixture.
5. After this, dip the broccoli florets in the cream mixture.
6. Then sprinkle every broccoli floret with the flour.
7. Preheat the air fryer to 400 F.
8. Put the broccoli florets in the air fryer tray.
9. Cook the broccoli for 5 minutes.
10. After this, shake the broccoli florets gently and cook them for 1 minute.
11. Then chill the broccoli gently and serve.
12. Enjoy!

Nutrition: calories 157, fat 6.8, fiber 4.6, carbs 18.4, protein 8.6

Dill Mashed Potato

Prep time: 10 minutes
Cooking time: 15 minutes
Servings: 2
Ingredients:

- 2 potatoes
- 2 tablespoon fresh dill, chopped
- 1 teaspoon butter
- ½ teaspoon salt
- ¼ cup half and half

Directions:

1. Preheat the air fryer to 390 F.
2. Wash the potatoes carefully and place them in the air fryer.
3. Cook the potatoes for 15 minutes.
4. After this, remove the potatoes from the air fryer.
5. Peel the potatoes.
6. Mash the potatoes with the help of the fork well.
7. Then add chopped fresh dill and salt.
8. Stir it gently and add butter and half and half.
9. Take the hand blender and blend the mixture well.
10. When the mashed potato is cooked – serve it immediately.
11. Enjoy!

Nutrition: calories 211, fat 5.7, fiber 5.5, carbs 36.5, protein 5.1

Butternut Squash Puree

Prep time: 10 minutes
Cooking time: 10 minutes
Servings: 2
Ingredients:

- ½ teaspoon salt
- 12 oz butternut squash
- ¼ cup water
- 2 tablespoon cream
- ¼ teaspoon sage
- ½ teaspoon butter, unsalted

Directions:

1. Chop the butternut squash and put it in the air fryer.
2. Add water and shake it gently.
3. Sprinkle the vegetables with the salt.
4. Set the air fryer to 400 F.
5. Cook the vegetables for 10 minutes.
6. Meanwhile, melt the butter and combine it with the cream.
7. Stir the mixture and add sage.
8. When the butternut squash is cooked – blend it well with the help of the hand blender.
9. Then add the cream mixture and stir it well with the help of the spoon.
10. Serve the side dish hot.
11. Enjoy!

Nutrition: calories 93, fat 1.8, fiber 3.4, carbs 20.3, protein 1.8

Cream Potato

Prep time: 15 minutes
Cooking time: 20 minutes
Servings: 2
Ingredients:

- 3 medium potatoes, scrubbed
- ½ teaspoon kosher salt
- 1 tablespoon Italian seasoning
- 1/3 cup cream
- ½ teaspoon ground black pepper

Directions:

1. Slice the potatoes.
2. Preheat the air fryer to 365 F.
3. Make the layer from the sliced potato in the air fryer basket.
4. Sprinkle the potato layer with the kosher salt and ground black pepper.
5. After this, make the second layer of the potato and sprinkle it with Italian seasoning.
6. Make the last layer of the sliced potato and pour the cream.
7. Cook the scallop potato for 20 minutes.
8. When the scalloped potato is cooked – let it chill till the room temperature.
9. Enjoy!

Nutrition: calories 269, fat 4.7, fiber 7.8, carbs 52.6, protein 5.8

Tomato Nutmeg Zucchini

Prep time: 10 minutes
Cooking time: 8 minutes
Servings: 2
Ingredients:

- 1 zucchini
- ½ onion, diced
- 2 tablespoon tomato sauce
- 1 teaspoon olive oil
- ½ teaspoon ground black pepper
- ½ teaspoon salt
- 1 pinch ground nutmeg

Directions:

1. Wash the zucchini and grate it with the help of the grater.
2. After this, combine together the grated zucchini and diced onion.
3. Place the mixture in the air fryer tray.
4. Sprinkle it with the olive oil, ground black pepper, salt, and nutmeg.
5. Stir the zucchini mixture gently with the help of the wooden spatula.
6. Preheat the air fryer to 390 F.
7. Cook the zucchini mixture for 5 minutes.
8. After this, stir the zucchini mixture carefully and add the tomato sauce.
9. Mix it up and cook for 3 minutes more at 400 F.
10. When the meal is cooked – stir it gently one more time and chill to the room temperature.
11. Enjoy!

Nutrition: calories 52, fat 2.6, fiber 2.1, carbs 7.1, protein 1.8

Cabbage with Tomato

Prep time: 20 minutes
Cooking time: 10 minutes
Servings: 2
Ingredients:

- 1 teaspoon sugar
- 14 oz cabbage
- 1 yellow onion
- ½ carrot, grated
- 4 tablespoon chicken stock
- ¼ teaspoon sriracha
- 1 tablespoon dried cilantro
- 1/3 teaspoon salt
- ½ teaspoon turmeric
- 2 tablespoon fresh parsley, chopped
- 1 tablespoon olive oil
- ¼ cup tomato sauce
- 1 garlic clove, sliced

Directions:

1. Shred the cabbage and toss it in the bowl.
2. Sprinkle the shredded cabbage with the salt and turmeric.
3. Mix it up with the help of the hands and leave for 5 minutes.
4. Meanwhile, preheat the air fryer to 390 F.
5. Sprinkle the air fryer basket with the olive oil and place the cabbage there.
6. Sprinkle the cabbage with the grated carrot, chicken stock, sriracha, dried cilantro, turmeric, olive oil, and sliced garlic.
7. After this, add the tomato sauce and stir the cabbage carefully.
8. Cook it for 2 minutes.
9. Meanwhile, peel the yellow onion and dice it.
10. When the time is over – add the diced yellow onion in the air fryer basket,
11. Add sugar and fresh parsley. Stir the cabbage mixture carefully until homogenous.
12. Increase the temperature to 400 F and cook the meal for 5 minutes more.
13. After this, stir the cabbage meal carefully with the help of the wooden spatula and cook for 3 minutes more.
14. When the cabbage is cooked – let it rest for 10 minutes.
15. Enjoy!

Nutrition: calories 160, fat 7.5, fiber 7.3, carbs 23.1, protein 4

Oregano Garlic Heads

Prep time: 10 minutes
Cooking time: 10 minutes
Servings: 2
Ingredients:

- 2 garlic heads, (10 cloves)
- 1 teaspoon dried oregano
- ½ teaspoon dried parsley
- 2 tablespoon olive oil
- ¼ teaspoon ground black pepper
- ¼ teaspoon ground thyme
- ¼ teaspoon ground nutmeg

Directions:

1. Preheat the air fryer to 390 F.
2. Combine the dried oregano, dried parsley, ground black pepper, ground thyme, and ground nutmeg in the shallow bowl.
3. Shake the bowl gently to make the spice mixture homogenous.
4. After this, cut the ends of the garlic heads.
5. Rub the garlic heads with the spicy mixture.
6. Then sprinkle every garlic head with 1 tablespoon of olive oil.
7. Wrap the garlic heads in the foil and place them in the air fryer basket.
8. Cook the garlic heads for 10 minutes.
9. After this, let the cooked garlic heads chill gently.
10. Discard the foil from the garlic heads.
11. Serve it.

Nutrition: calories 192, fat 14.4, fiber 1.5, carbs 15.8, protein 3

Feta Beet Cubes

Prep time: 10 minutes
Cooking time: 12 minutes
Servings: 2
Ingredients:

- 2 small beets
- ½ teaspoon salt
- 3 oz Feta cheese
- 1 tablespoon olive oil
- ½ teaspoon sesame oil
- ¼ teaspoon dried oregano
- 1/3 teaspoon dried thyme
- 1 teaspoon fresh celery, chopped

Directions:

1. Peel the beets and cut into the medium cubes.
2. Put the beet cubes in the bowl and sprinkle with salt, dried oregano, and dried thyme.
3. Shake the beets gently.
4. Preheat the air fryer to 365 F.
5. Sprinkle the beet cubes with the olive oil and shake well.
6. After this, put the beet cubes in the air fryer basket and cook for 12 minutes or until the beets are tender.
7. Transfer the cooked beets to the serving bowl.
8. Add the chopped fresh celery and sesame oil.
9. Then scramble Feta cheese over the beets.
10. Enjoy!

Nutrition: calories 227, fat 17.4, fiber 2.2, carbs 12, protein 7.8

Eggplant & Zucchini Mix

Prep time: 15 minutes
Cooking time: 14 minutes
Servings: 2
Ingredients:

- 1 eggplant
- 1 zucchini
- 1 red sweet pepper
- 2 oz green beans
- ½ apple
- 1 tomato
- 1 tablespoon Italian seasoning
- 2 tablespoon olive oil
- ½ teaspoon ground black pepper
- 1 teaspoon salt
- 1 tablespoon fresh lemon juice
- 1 teaspoon butter
- ½ white onion, sliced
- 1 tablespoon tomato sauce
- 1 garlic clove, peeled
- ¼ teaspoon sage

Directions:

1. Peel the eggplants and chop it.
2. Chop the zucchini into the same pieces as the eggplant.
3. After this, discard the seeds from the sweet pepper and chop it.
4. Place all the vegetables in the mixing bowl.
5. Add green beans.
6. Chop the apple and add it to the mixture too.
7. After this, chop the tomato and add it to the vegetable mixture.
8. Sprinkle the vegetables with the olive oil, Italian seasoning, ground black pepper, salt, fresh lemon juice, sliced onion, tomato sauce, and sage.
9. Slice the garlic clove and sprinkle over the vegetable mixture.
10. Then toss the butter in the air fryer and preheat it to 370 F.
11. When the butter is melted – transfer the vegetable mixture to the air fryer basket.
12. Cook the vegetables for 7 minutes.
13. After this, shake the vegetables carefully.
14. Cook the meal for 7 minutes more.
15. When all the vegetables are tender – the meal is cooked.
16. Shake it one more time and transfer to the serving plates.
17. Enjoy!

Nutrition: calories 312, fat 19.1, fiber 13.6, carbs 37, protein 5.7

Chard with Cheddar

Prep time: 10 minutes
Cooking time: 11 minutes
Servings: 2
Ingredients:

- 3 oz Cheddar cheese, grated
- 10 oz Swiss chard
- 3 tablespoon cream
- 1 tablespoon sesame oil
- ½ teaspoon salt
- ½ teaspoon ground white pepper

Directions:

1. Wash Swiss chard carefully and chop it roughly.
2. After this, sprinkle chopped Swiss chard with the salt and ground white pepper.
3. Stir it carefully.
4. Sprinkle Swiss chard with the sesame oil and stir it carefully with the help of 2 spatulas.
5. Preheat the air fryer to 260 F.
6. Put chopped Swiss chard in the air fryer basket and cook for 6 minutes.
7. Shake it after 3 minutes of cooking.
8. Then pour the cream into the air fryer basket and mix it up.
9. Cook the meal for 3 minutes more.
10. Then increase the temperature to 400 F.
11. Sprinkle the meal with the grated cheese and cook for 2 minutes more.
12. After this, transfer the meal in the serving plates.
13. Enjoy!

Nutrition: calories 272, fat 22.3, fiber 2.5, carbs 6.7, protein 13.3

Sweet Potato Cubes

Prep time: 10 minutes
Cooking time: 13 minutes
Servings: 2
Ingredients:

- 2 sweet potatoes (yum)
- 1 tablespoon olive oil
- ½ teaspoon ground thyme
- ¼ teaspoon chili flakes
- 1/3 teaspoon salt
- ½ teaspoon butter

Directions:

1. Peel the sweet potatoes and cut them into the medium cubes.
2. Then combine together the chili flakes, salt, and ground thyme.
3. Melt the butter and combine it with the olive oil.
4. Add the spice mixture and churn it.
5. Sprinkle the sweet potato cubes with the churned olive oil mixture.
6. Shake it well.
7. Preheat the air fryer to 360 F.
8. Put the sweet potato cubes in the air fryer basket and cook for 10 minutes.
9. Shake the meal well and cook for 3 minutes more.
10. When the sweet potato is tender – it is cooked.
11. Let it chill gently.
12. Serve it!

Nutrition: calories 70, fat 8, fiber 0.1, carbs 0.5, protein 0.1

Sweet Onion Rings

Prep time: 10 minutes
Cooking time: 5 minutes
Servings: 2
Ingredients:

- 2 white onions
- 1 tablespoon brown sugar
- 1 pinch salt
- ¼ teaspoon turmeric
- 1 teaspoon olive oil
- 1 tablespoon cornstarch

Directions:

1. Peel the onions and cut them into the thick rings.
2. Then combine together the brown sugar and salt.
3. Add turmeric and cornstarch.
4. Mix it up.
5. Put the onion rings in a bowl and sprinkle them generously with the brown sugar mixture.
6. Preheat the air fryer to 400 F.
7. Put the onion rings in the air fryer basket and sprinkle with the olive oil.
8. Shake them gently and cook for 5 minutes.
9. Shake the onion rings after 3 minutes of cooking. The cooked onion rings should not be crunchy.
10. Serve the meal immediately.
11. Enjoy!

Nutrition: calories 77, fat 0.1, fiber 2.5, carbs 18.5, protein 1.3

Olive Oil Okra

Prep time: 10 minutes
Cooking time: 7 minutes
Servings: 2
Ingredients:

- 1 teaspoon garlic powder
- 4 garlic cloves
- 10 oz okra
- 1 teaspoon olive oil
- ½ teaspoon salt
- 1 egg
- ¼ teaspoon ground black pepper

Directions:

1. Crack the egg into the bowl and whisk it.
2. Sprinkle the whisked egg with the salt and ground black pepper.
3. Then add the garlic powder and stir it carefully.
4. Mince the garlic cloves and add them to the egg mixture. Stir it gently.
5. Put the okra in the egg mixture and mix up it.
6. Preheat the air fryer to 400 F.
7. Put the okra in the air fryer basket and cook it for 7 minutes.
8. Shake okra after 5 minutes of cooking.
9. Then let the cooked meal chill little.
10. Serve it!

Nutrition: calories 122, fat 4.8, fiber 4.9, carbs 13.9, protein 6.2

Mushrooms & Cream

Prep time: 10 minutes
Cooking time: 8 minutes
Servings: 2
Ingredients:

- 9 oz mushrooms
- 3 tablespoon cream
- 1 teaspoon flour
- ¼ teaspoon ground black pepper
- ¼ teaspoon salt
- ½ onion, grated
- 1 tablespoon butter
- ¼ green chili, chopped

Directions:

1. Wash the mushrooms and slice them.
2. Sprinkle the mushrooms with ground black pepper and salt.
3. Stir the mixture.
4. Preheat the air fryer to 360 F.
5. Toss the butter in the air fryer basket and melt it.
6. When the butter is melted – add the sliced mushrooms in the air fryer.
7. Stir the mushrooms and cook them for 5 minutes.
8. Meanwhile, combine together flour, cream, and grated onion
9. Add chili pepper and whisk it until homogenous.
10. Then pour the cream mixture over the mushrooms and stir it.
11. Increase the temperature to 400 F and cook the meal for 3 minutes more.
12. Then stir the meal carefully and serve it.
13. Enjoy!

Nutrition: calories 106, fat 7.2, fiber 2, carbs 8.5, protein 4.7

Mexican Parmesan Corn

Prep time: 5 minutes
Cooking time: 13 minutes
Servings: 2
Ingredients:

- 1 tablespoon green chili powder
- 2 tablespoon mayonnaise
- 2 corn on cobs
- 3 oz Parmesan, shredded
- ½ teaspoon salt
- 1/3 teaspoon olive oil

Directions:

1. Preheat the air fryer to 365 F.
2. Sprinkle the corn with the salt and olive oil.
3. Put the rack in the air fryer.
4. Place the corn on the cobs on the rack and cook it for 13 minutes.
5. Then remove the corn from the cobs from the air fryer and brush it with the mayonnaise from all sides.
6. Combine together the green chili powder and shredded Parmesan.
7. Then sprinkle the corn with the cheese mixture.
8. Enjoy!

Nutrition: calories 213, fat 15.4, fiber 1.3, carbs 7.3, protein 14.3

Tahini Eggplants

Prep time: 20 minutes
Cooking time: 15 minutes
Servings: 2
Ingredients:

- 1 teaspoon tahini
- 2 tablespoon soy sauce
- 3 tablespoon fresh lemon juice
- ½ teaspoon sesame seeds
- ¼ teaspoon salt
- ½ teaspoon brown sugar
- 1 tablespoon olive oil
- 2 eggplants
- 1 garlic clove, chopped
- ½ teaspoon garlic powder

Directions:

1. Peel the eggplants and chop them roughly.
2. Combine together the soy sauce and fresh lemon juice.
3. Sprinkle the chopped eggplants with the soy-lemon mixture.
4. Then sprinkle the vegetables with the salt, brown sugar, chopped garlic clove, and garlic powder.
5. Add tahini and mix it up.
6. Leave the eggplants mixture for 15 minutes in the fridge.
7. Preheat the air fryer to 400 F.
8. Put the eggplants and remaining liquid from the eggplants in the air fryer basket.
9. Cook the vegetables for 15 minutes.
10. Shake the eggplants every 4 minutes.
11. When the eggplants cooked – shake them one more time and sprinkle with the sesame seeds and olive oil.
12. Stir the eggplants and serve.
13. Enjoy!

Nutrition: calories 238, fat 9.9, fiber 20, carbs 36.4, protein 7.3

Cream Cheese Cauliflower

Prep time: 10 minutes
Cooking time: 12 minutes
Servings: 2
Ingredients:

- 1 teaspoon tahini
- 1/3 cup cream
- 13 oz cauliflower
- ½ onion, diced, sautéed
- ½ teaspoon salt
- ½ teaspoon garlic powder
- 1 teaspoon cream cheese
- ½ teaspoon butter

Directions:

1. Wash the cauliflower carefully and chop it.
2. Sprinkle the chopped cauliflower with the salt and garlic powder.
3. Shake the mixture.
4. Preheat the air fryer to 400 F.
5. Put the cauliflower in the air fryer basket.
6. Add cream and cream cheese.
7. After this, add butter and shake the mixture gently.
8. Cook the cauliflower for 12 minutes.
9. Shake the cauliflower after 6 minutes of cooking.
10. Then transfer the cooked cauliflower to the mixing bowl.
11. Blend it well with the help of the hand blender.
12. When the mixture is smooth – add sautéed onion and mix up it.
13. Serve the meal warm.
14. Enjoy!

Nutrition: calories 114, fat 5.3, fiber 5.5, carbs 14.7, protein 5

Feta Cheese Potato Slices

Prep time: 10 minutes
Cooking time: 14 minutes
Servings: 2
Ingredients:

- 1 egg
- 3 oz Feta cheese, scrambled
- 4 potatoes
- ½ teaspoon salt
- 1 tablespoon butter
- ¼ teaspoon paprika
- ½ teaspoon ground black pepper
- ½ teaspoon turmeric
- 2 tablespoon cream

Directions:

1. Peel the potatoes and slice them.
2. Sprinkle the sliced potatoes with the salt, paprika, ground black pepper, and turmeric.
3. Mix the potatoes.
4. Preheat the air fryer to 390 F.
5. Toss the butter in the air fryer basket and melt it.
6. Then place the potato slices in the air fryer basket.
7. Beat the egg and whisk it.
8. Pour the whisked egg over the potatoes.
9. Add cream and cook the potatoes for 10 minutes.
10. Then sprinkle the potatoes with Feta cheese and cook potato for 4 minutes more.
11. When the meal is cooked – let it chill till the room temperature and serve.
12. Enjoy!

Nutrition: calories 500, fat 18.2, fiber 10.6, carbs 70, protein 16.3

Thyme Fennel

Prep time: 10 minutes
Cooking time: 10 minutes
Servings: 2
Ingredients:

- 1 tablespoon thyme
- 12 oz fennel
- 1 tablespoon brown sugar
- 1 tablespoon butter
- ½ teaspoon olive oil
- 1 pinch salt
- 1 pinch ground black pepper
- ½ teaspoon chili flakes

Directions:

1. Preheat the air fryer to 365 F.
2. Chop the fennel roughly.
3. Sprinkle the fennel with the salt, ground black pepper, and chili flakes.
4. Mix the mixture.
5. Sprinkle the fennel with the olive oil and place in the air fryer.
6. Cook the fennel for 8 minutes. Flip the fennel after 4 minutes of the cooking.
7. Meanwhile, melt the butter and combine it together with the thyme and brown sugar.
8. Whisk the mixture until the sugar is dissolved.
9. Then sprinkle the fennel with the sugar mixture and cook for 2 minutes more.
10. Serve the cooked meal immediately.
11. Enjoy!

Nutrition: calories 135, fat 7.4, fiber 5.8, carbs 17.7, protein 2.3

Chili Squash Wedges

Prep time: 10 minutes
Cooking time: 18 minutes
Servings: 2
Ingredients:

- 11 oz Acorn squash
- ½ teaspoon salt
- 1 tablespoon olive oil
- ½ teaspoon chili pepper
- ½ teaspoon paprika

Directions:

1. Cut Acorn squash into the serving wedges.
2. Sprinkle the wedges with the salt, olive oil, chili pepper, and paprika.
3. Massage the wedges gently.
4. Preheat the air fryer to 400 F.
5. Put Acorn squash wedges in the air fryer basket and cook for 18 minutes.
6. Flip the wedges into another side after 9 minutes of cooking.
7. Serve the cooked meal hot.
8. Enjoy!

Nutrition: calories 125, fat 7.2, fiber 2.6, carbs 16.7, protein 1.4

Paprika Yellow Squash

Prep time: 10 minutes
Cooking time: 12 minutes
Servings: 2
Ingredients:

- 10 oz yellow squash
- 1 yellow onion
- ¼ cup chicken stock
- 1 tablespoon olive oil
- ¼ teaspoon paprika
- ¼ teaspoon salt
- ½ teaspoon ground black pepper
- 1 tablespoon mayonnaise
- 3 teaspoon lemon juice
- 2 oz Cheddar, shredded

Directions:

1. Chop the yellow squash and put it in the bowl.
2. Sprinkle the yellow squash with the chicken stock, olive oil, paprika, salt, and ground black pepper.
3. Shake the vegetables carefully.
4. Then preheat the air fryer to 390 F.
5. Put the yellow squash in the air fryer basket and cook for 7 minutes.
6. After this, shake the yellow squash.
7. Combine together the mayonnaise with fresh lemon juice and shredded cheese.
8. Put the mayonnaise mixture in the air fryer and mix it up.
9. Cook the meal at 400 F for 4 minutes more.
10. Then mix the meal carefully and serve it immediately.
11. Enjoy!

Nutrition: calories 188, fat 11.9, fiber 3, carbs 12.9, protein 9.6

Puff Cauliflower Patties

Prep time: 10 minutes
Cooking time: 9 minutes
Servings: 2
Ingredients:

- 3 oz puff pastry
- 7 oz mashed cauliflower
- 1 egg yolk
- ½ teaspoon cumin
- ¼ teaspoon salt
- 1 oz carrot, sautéed

Directions:

1. Roll the puff pastry and cut it into the triangles.
2. Then combine the sautéed carrot with the mashed cauliflower.
3. Place the filing on the triangles and secure them well.
4. Whisk the egg and brush the patties.
5. Sprinkle the patties with the cumin and salt.
6. Preheat the air fryer to 390 F.
7. Put the patties on the air fryer rack and cook for 9 minutes.
8. When the patties are golden brown – they are cooked.
9. Transfer them to the serving plates.
10. Enjoy!

Nutrition: calories 333, fat 24.4, fiber 2.8, carbs 23.4, protein 6.4

Cottage Cheese Mushrooms

Prep time: 10 minutes
Cooking time: 6 minutes
Servings: 2
Ingredients:

- 3 oz Parmesan, shredded
- 3 oz cottage cheese
- 2 tablespoon fresh parsley, chopped
- ¼ teaspoon minced garlic
- ½ teaspoon butter
- 2 Portobello mushroom hats
- 1/3 teaspoon salt

Directions:

1. Peel the mushroom hats.
2. Combine together chopped parsley, minced garlic, cottage cheese, salt, and butter.
3. Mix it with the help of the hand blender.
4. Preheat the air fryer to 400 F.
5. Fill the mushrooms with the cottage cheese mixture and put them in the air fryer basket.
6. Cook the mushrooms for 4 minutes.
7. Then sprinkle the mushrooms with the shredded cheese and cook for 2 minutes more.
8. Let the cooked mushrooms chill gently.
9. Serve the meal!

Nutrition: calories 205, fat 10.9, fiber 1.1, carbs 6.4, protein 22.7

Honey Carrots with Greens

Prep time: 7 minutes
Cooking time: 12 minutes
Servings: 2
Ingredients:

- 1 cup baby carrot
- ½ teaspoon salt
- ½ teaspoon white pepper
- 1 tablespoon honey
- 1 teaspoon sesame oil

Directions:

1. Preheat the air fryer to 385 F.
2. Combine the baby carrot with the salt, white pepper, and sesame oil.
3. Shake the baby carrot and transfer in the air fryer basket.
4. Cook the vegetables for 10 minutes.
5. After this, add honey and shake the vegetables.
6. Cook the meal for 2 minutes.
7. After this, shake the vegetables and serve immediately.
8. Enjoy!

Nutrition: calories 83, fat 2.4, fiber 2.6, carbs 16, protein 0.6

Creamy Red Potatoes

Prep time: 15 minutes
Cooking time: 10 minutes
Servings: 2
Ingredients:

- 4 red potatoes
- ¼ cup cream cheese
- ½ tablespoon onion powder
- 4 tablespoon chicken stock
- ½ teaspoon salt
- 1 tablespoon butter
- ½ teaspoon olive oil

Directions:

1. Wash the potatoes and peel them.
2. Chop the potatoes roughly and sprinkle with the olive oil and salt.
3. Preheat the air fryer to 400 F.
4. Put the potato in the air fryer basket and add butter.
5. Cook the potato for 10 minutes.
6. Shake the potato after 7 minutes of cooking.
7. After this, smash the potatoes with the help of the fork.
8. Add onion powder, chicken stock, and cream cheese.
9. Mix the potatoes until homogenous and serve.
10. Taste it!

Nutrition: calories 468, fat 17.7, fiber 7.3, carbs 70, protein 10.6

Snacks and Appetizers

Sesame Tofu Cubes

Prep time: 20 minutes
Cooking time: 20 minutes
Servings: 2
Ingredients:

- 8 oz tofu
- 1 teaspoon cornstarch
- 1 teaspoon scallions, chopped
- 1 teaspoon rice vinegar
- 1 teaspoon sesame oil
- 1 teaspoon soy sauce

Directions:

1. Cut the tofu into the cubes.
2. Put the tofu cubes in the bowl and sprinkle with the rice vinegar, sesame oil, and soy sauce.
3. Shake the mixture.
4. Leave the tofu for 10 minutes to marinate.
5. Preheat the air fryer to 370 F.
6. Sprinkle the marinated tofu with the cornstarch and put in the air fryer basket.
7. Cook tofu for 20 minutes.
8. Shake the tofu after 11 minutes of cooking.
9. Then chill the tofu gently and sprinkle with the chopped scallions.
10. Enjoy!

Nutrition: calories 108, fat 7, fiber 1.1, carbs 3.4, protein 9.5

Thyme Salty Tomatoes

Prep time: 10 minutes
Cooking time: 10 minutes
Servings: 2
Ingredients:

- 2 tomatoes
- 1 tablespoon thyme
- 1 pinch salt
- 1 teaspoon olive oil

Directions:

1. Preheat the air fryer to 375 F.
2. Slice the tomatoes.
3. Then combine together thyme and salt. Shake the mixture.
4. Sprinkle the sliced tomatoes with the thyme mixture.
5. Place the sliced tomatoes in the air fryer and spray with the olive oil.
6. Cook the tomatoes for 10 minutes.
7. When the tomatoes are cooked – they should have tender and little bit dry texture.
8. Enjoy!

Nutrition: calories 46, fat 2.7, fiber 2, carbs 5.6, protein 1.2

Creamy Chicken Liver

Prep time: 10 minutes
Cooking time: 10 minutes
Servings: 2
Ingredients:

- 7 oz chicken liver
- ¼ cup water
- 1 tablespoon butter
- 2 teaspoon cream
- 1 tablespoon fresh dill, chopped
- 1 pinch salt

Directions:

1. Preheat the air fryer to 390 F.
2. Combine together water, chicken liver, and salt.
3. Mix the mixture and place it in the air fryer basket.
4. Cook the chicken liver for 10 minutes.
5. Stir it after 5 minutes of cooking.
6. Then transfer the cooked chicken liver to the bowl.
7. Add cream and butter.
8. Blend the mixture until smooth.
9. After this, add chopped fresh dill and stir gently.
10. Serve the meal and enjoy!

Nutrition: calories 223, fat 12.5, fiber 0.2, carbs 1.9, protein 24.7

Catfish Sticks

Prep time: 10 minutes
Cooking time: 10 minutes
Servings: 2
Ingredients:

- 8 oz catfish fillet
- ½ teaspoon salt
- ½ teaspoon ground black pepper
- ¼ cup panko breadcrumbs
- 1 egg
- ½ teaspoon olive oil

Directions:

1. Cut the catfish fillet into 2 medium pieces (sticks).
2. Then sprinkle the catfish with the salt and ground black pepper.
3. Beat the egg in the bowl and whisk it.
4. Dip the catfish fillets in the whisked egg.
5. After this, coat the fish in the panko breadcrumbs.
6. Preheat the air fryer to 380 F.
7. Put the fish sticks in the air fryer basket and spray with the olive oil.
8. Cook the fish sticks for 10 minutes.
9. Flip the sticks into another side after 10 minutes of cooking.
10. When the fish sticks are cooked – let them chill gently.
11. Serve the meal!

Nutrition: calories 231, fat 12.2, fiber 1.1, carbs 8, protein 21.5

Honey Banana Chips

Prep time: 10 minutes
Cooking time: 6 minutes
Servings: 2
Ingredients:

- 2 bananas
- 1 teaspoon honey
- 1 pinch white pepper
- ½ teaspoon olive oil

Directions:

1. Peel the bananas and slice them into the chips pieces.
2. Then sprinkle the bananas with the honey and white pepper.
3. Spray the olive oil over the bananas and mix them gently with the help of the hands.
4. Preheat the air fryer to 320 F.
5. Put the banana chips in the air fryer basket and cook for 6 minutes.
6. Serve the cooked banana chips immediately.
7. Enjoy!

Nutrition: calories 126, fat 1.6, fiber 3.1, carbs 29.9, protein 1.3

Ginger Apple Chips

Prep time: 8 minutes
Cooking time: 10 minutes
Servings: 2
Ingredients:

- ½ teaspoon olive oil
- 3 apples
- 1 pinch ground ginger

Directions:

1. Peel the apples and remove the seeds.
2. Slice the apples and sprinkle them with the ground ginger and olive oil.
3. Preheat the air fryer to 400 F.
4. Place the apple slices on the air fryer rack.
5. Cook the apple chips for 10 minutes.
6. Shake the apple chips carefully after 4 minutes of cooking.
7. Then chill the apple chips carefully.
8. Serve the meal immediately or keep it in the paper bag in the dry place.
9. Enjoy!

Nutrition: calories 184, fat 1.8, fiber 8.1, carbs 46.3, protein 0.9

Maple Carrot Fries

Prep time: 5 minutes
Cooking time: 10 minutes
Servings: 2
Ingredients:

- 1 cup baby carrot
- ¼ cup maple syrup
- 1 pinch salt
- ½ teaspoon thyme
- ½ teaspoon ground black pepper
- 1 teaspoon dried oregano
- 1 tablespoon olive oil

Directions:

1. Preheat the air fryer to 410 F.
2. Place the baby carrot in the air fryer basket.
3. Sprinkle the baby carrot with the thyme, salt, ground black pepper, and dried oregano.
4. Then spray the olive oil over the baby carrot and shake it well.
5. Cook the baby carrot fries for 10 minutes.
6. Shake the carrot fries after 6 minutes of cooking.
7. Chill the cooked meal for 5 minutes.
8. Enjoy!

Nutrition: calories 197, fat 7.3, fiber 3, carbs 34.4, protein 0.7

Sweet Potato Fries

Prep time: 10 minutes
Cooking time: 15 minutes
Servings: 2
Ingredients:

- 2 sweet potatoes
- 1 tablespoon coconut oil
- 1/3 teaspoon salt
- ½ teaspoon ground black pepper
- ½ teaspoon onion powder

Directions:

1. Preheat the air fryer to 370 F.
2. Peel the sweet potatoes and cut them into the fries.
3. Sprinkle the vegetables with the salt, ground black pepper, and onion powder.
4. Shake the sweet potatoes and sprinkle with the coconut oil.
5. Put the uncooked sweet potato fries in the air fryer basket and cook for 15 minutes.
6. Shake the sweet potato fries every 5 minutes.
7. When the sweet potato fries are cooked – let them chill gently.
8. Serve the meal!

Nutrition: calories 225, fat 6.8, fiber 5.2, carbs 42.1, protein 2.6

Squid Rings

Prep time: 10 minutes
Cooking time: 4 minutes
Servings: 2
Ingredients:

- 2 squid tubes
- 2 eggs
- 1/3 cup flour
- ¼ teaspoon salt
- ½ teaspoon onion powder
- ½ teaspoon garlic powder

Directions:

1. Wash and peel the squid cubes carefully.
2. Then slice the squid cubes into the rings.
3. Beat the eggs in the bowl and whisk them.
4. Then dip the squid rings in the whisked eggs.
5. Combine together flour, salt, onion powder, and garlic powder. Stir the mixture with the help of the fork.
6. Then coat the squid rings with the flour mixture.
7. Preheat the air fryer to 400 F.
8. Put the squid rings onto the air fryer rack.
9. Cook the squid rings for 4 minutes.
10. Shake the squid rings after 3 minutes of cooking.
11. When the squid rings are cooked – let them chill till the room temperature.
12. Enjoy!

Nutrition: calories 383, fat 10.5, fiber 0.7, carbs 17.2, protein 55.8

Carrot Chips

Prep time: 10 minutes
Cooking time: 20 minutes
Servings: 2
Ingredients:

- 3 carrots
- ½ teaspoon salt
- ½ teaspoon ground black pepper
- 1 tablespoon canola oil

Directions:

1. Peel the carrot and slice into the chips.
2. Then sprinkle the uncooked carrot chips with the salt, ground black pepper, and canola oil.
3. Shake the carrot chips carefully.
4. Preheat the air fryer to 360 F.
5. Put the carrot chips in the air fryer basket.
6. Shake the carrot chips in halfway.
7. Check the doneness of the carrot chips while cooking.
8. Chill the carrot chips and serve.
9. Enjoy!

Nutrition: calories 101, fat 7, fiber 2.4, carbs 9.3, protein 0.8

Corn Okra Bites

Prep time: 10 minutes
Cooking time: 4 minutes
Servings: 2
Ingredients:

- 4 tablespoon corn flakes, crushed
- 9 oz okra
- 1 egg
- ½ teaspoon salt
- 1 teaspoon olive oil

Directions:

1. Preheat the air fryer to 400 F.
2. Chop the okra roughly.
3. Combine together the corn flakes and salt.
4. Crack the egg into the bowl and whisk it.
5. Toss the chopped okra in the whisked egg.
6. Then coat the chopped okra with the corn flakes.
7. Put the chopped okra in the air fryer basket and sprinkle with the olive oil.
8. Cook the okra for 4 minutes.
9. Shake the okra after 2 minutes of cooking.
10. When the okra is cooked – let it chill gently.
11. Enjoy!

Nutrition: calories 115, fat 4.8, fiber 4.2, carbs 12.7, protein 5.2

Salty Potato Chips

Prep time: 10 minutes
Cooking time: 19 minutes
Servings: 2
Ingredients:

- 3 potatoes
- 1 tablespoon canola oil
- ½ teaspoon salt

Directions:

1. Wash the potatoes carefully and do not peel them.
2. Slice the potatoes into the chips.
3. Sprinkle the potato chips with the olive oil and salt.
4. Mix the potatoes carefully.
5. Preheat the air fryer to 400 F.
6. Put the potato chips in the air fryer basket and cook for 19 minutes.
7. Shake the potato chips every 3 minutes.
8. When the potato chips are cooked – chill them well.
9. Enjoy!

Nutrition: calories 282, fat 7.3, fiber 7.7, carbs 50.2, protein 5.4

Corn & Beans Fries

Prep time: 10 minutes
Cooking time: 7 minutes
Servings: 2
Ingredients:

- ¼ cup corn flakes crumbs
- 1 egg
- 10 oz green beans
- 1 tablespoon canola oil
- ½ teaspoon salt
- 1 teaspoon garlic powder

Directions:

1. Preheat the air fryer to 400 F.
2. Put the green beans in the bowl.
3. Beat the egg in the green beans and stir carefully until homogenous.
4. Then sprinkle the green beans with the salt and garlic powder.
5. Shake gently.
6. Then coat the green beans in the corn flakes crumbs well.
7. Put the green beans in the air fryer basket in one layer.
8. Cook the green beans for 7 minutes.
9. Shake the green beans twice during the cooking.
10. When the green beans are cooked – let them chill and serve.
11. Enjoy!

Nutrition: calories 182, fat 9.4, fiber 5.3, carbs 21, protein 6.3

Sugary Apple Fritters

Prep time: 10 minutes
Cooking time: 8 minutes
Servings: 2
Ingredients:

- 2 red apples
- 1 teaspoon sugar
- 1 tablespoon flour
- 1 tablespoon semolina
- 1 teaspoon lemon juice
- ½ teaspoon ground cinnamon
- 1 teaspoon butter
- 1 egg

Directions:

1. Peel the apples and grate them.
2. Sprinkle the grated apples with the lemon juice.
3. Then add sugar, flour, semolina, and ground cinnamon.
4. Mix the mixture and crack the egg.
5. Mix the apple mixture carefully.
6. Preheat the air fryer to 370 F.
7. Toss the butter in the air fryer basket and melt it.
8. When the butter is melted – make the medium fritters from the apple mixture. Use 2 spoons for this step.
9. Place the fritters in the air fryer basket and cook for 6 minutes.
10. After this, flip the fritters to another side and cook for 2 minutes more.
11. Dry the cooked fritters with the help of the paper towel and serve.
12. Enjoy!

Nutrition: calories 207, fat 4.6, fiber 6, carbs 40.3, protein 4.5

Oregano Onion Rings

Prep time: 15 minutes
Cooking time: minutes
Servings: 2
Ingredients:

- 1 tablespoon oregano
- 1 tablespoon flour
- ½ teaspoon cornstarch
- 1 egg
- ½ teaspoon salt
- 2 white onions, peeled
- 1 tablespoon olive oil

Directions:

1. Crack the egg into the bowl and whisk it.
2. Combine together the flour and cornstarch in the separate bowl.
3. Add oregano and salt. Shake the mixture gently.
4. Peel the onions and slice them to get the "rings".
5. Then dip the onion rings in the whisked egg.
6. After this, coat the onion rings in the flour mixture.
7. Preheat the air fryer to 365 F.
8. Spray the air fryer basket with the olive oil inside.
9. Then place the onion rings in the air fryer and cook for 8 minutes.
10. Shake the onion rings after 4 minutes of cooking.
11. Let the cooked meal chill gently.
12. Serve it!

Nutrition: calories 159, fat 9.6, fiber 3.4, carbs 15.5, protein 4.6

Chili Bacon Slices

Prep time: 5 minutes
Cooking time: 11 minutes
Servings: 2
Ingredients:

- 1 tablespoon maple syrup
- 6 bacon slices
- ¼ teaspoon salt
- ¼ teaspoon chili flakes

Directions:

1. Rub the bacon slices with the salt and chili flakes.
2. Preheat the air fryer to 365 F.
3. Put the bacon slices on the air fryer rack and cook for 6 minutes.
4. After this, flip the bacon slices on another side and sprinkle with the maple syrup.
5. Cook the bacon slices for 5 minutes more.
6. When the bacon is crunchy – it is cooked.
7. Serve it immediately!

Nutrition: calories 335, fat 23.8, fiber 0, carbs 7.5, protein 21.1

Pepper Green Tomatoes

Prep time: 10 minutes
Cooking time: 18 minutes
Servings: 2
Ingredients:

- 4 green tomatoes
- 1 egg
- ¼ cup flour
- 1/3 teaspoon salt
- ½ teaspoon ground black pepper
- ¼ tablespoon olive oil

Directions:

1. Wash the green tomatoes and slice them.
2. Beat the egg in the bowl and whisk it.
3. Combine together the whisked egg and flour.
4. Add salt and ground black pepper. Stir the mixture well.
5. After this, dip the tomato slices in the whisked egg mixture.
6. Preheat the air fryer to 360 F.
7. Put the green tomatoes on air fryer rack and cook for 18 minutes.
8. Flip the tomatoes in the halfway mark.
9. Let the cooked meal chill till the room temperature.
10. Enjoy!

Nutrition: calories 149, fat 4.6, fiber 3.5, carbs 22, protein 6.6

Avocado Sushi

Prep time: 15 minutes
Cooking time: 4 minutes
Servings: 2
Ingredients:

- 1 sheet sushi nori
- ½ teaspoon garlic powder
- 2 teaspoon soy sauce
- ¼ teaspoon rice vinegar
- 1 teaspoon sesame seeds, roasted
- 5 oz sushi salmon
- 5 oz sushi rice, cooked
- 2 oz avocado
- ¼ cup panko breadcrumbs
- 1 tablespoon mayo sauce

Directions:

1. Combine the sushi rice with the soy sauce and rice vinegar.
2. Stir the mixture.
3. Then spread the sushi nori with the rice.
4. After this, cut the avocado into the strips.
5. Put the avocado strips in the center of the sushi nori.
6. Then add salmon.
7. Sprinkle the salmon with the garlic powder and sesame seeds.
8. Roll the sushi nori to make the shape of a stick.
9. After this, spread the sushi stick with the mayo sauce well.
10. Preheat the air fryer to 400 F.
11. Coat the sushi stick in the panko breadcrumbs and place in the air fryer rack.
12. Cook the sushi for 4 minutes. Flip the sushi stick after 2 minutes of cooking.
13. Then slice sushi into 6 pieces.
14. Enjoy!

Nutrition: calories 453, fat 9.5, fiber 4.6, carbs 67.9, protein 21.9

Mayo Cauliflower Florets

Prep time: 15 minutes
Cooking time: 12 minutes
Servings: 2
Ingredients:

- 1 tablespoon Buffalo sauce
- 1 tablespoon mayo sauce
- 1 tablespoon butter, melted
- 1 pinch salt
- 9 oz cauliflower florets
- ¼ cup panko breadcrumbs, Italian seasoned

Directions:

1. Combine together the melted butter, Buffalo sauce, and mayo sauce.
2. Whisk the mixture well.
3. Add salt and stir it gently.
4. Then coat the cauliflower florets in Buffalo sauce mixture well.
5. Preheat the air fryer to 360 F.
6. Transfer Buffalo cauliflower in the air fryer basket and cook for 12 minutes,
7. Shake the cauliflower after 7 minutes of cooking.
8. When the meal is cooked – chill it for 2-3 minutes and serve.
9. Enjoy!

Nutrition: calories 189, fat 13, fiber 3.9, carbs 16.3, protein 4.1

Smoked Cashews

Prep time: 8 minutes
Cooking time: 8 minutes
Servings: 2
Ingredients:

- 1 teaspoon liquid smoke
- 8 oz raw cashews
- ¼ teaspoon salt
- ¼ teaspoon sugar

Directions:

1. Put the raw cashews in the bowl.
2. Add liquid smoke, salt, and sugar.
3. Shake the mixture well.
4. After this, preheat the air fryer to 350 F.
5. Put the cashews in the air fryer basket and cook for 8 minutes.
6. Shake the cashews every 2 minutes of cooking.
7. Cook the cashews 1 extra minute if desired.
8. Then chill the cashews to the room temperature.
9. Serve the meal!

Nutrition: calories 653, fat 52.6, fiber 3.4, carbs 37.6, protein 17.4

Toasted Salty Walnuts

Prep time: 5 minutes
Cooking time: 5 minutes
Servings: 2
Ingredients:

- 1 teaspoon salt
- 5 oz walnuts
- ¼ teaspoon chili flakes
- ½ teaspoon ground nutmeg

Directions:

1. Preheat the air fryer to 350 F.
2. Put the walnuts in the air fryer basket.
3. Sprinkle the walnuts with the chili flakes and salt.
4. Add ground nutmeg and shake the walnuts.
5. Cook the walnuts for 3 minutes.
6. After this, increase the temperature to 360 F.
7. Shake the walnuts carefully and cook for 2 minutes more.
8. Then shake the walnuts and chill them.
9. Serve the meal and enjoy!

Nutrition: calories 441, fat 42, fiber 4.9, carbs 7.3, protein 17.1

Cinnamon Dough Bites

Prep time: 10 minutes
Cooking time: 6 minutes
Servings: 2
Ingredients:

- 4 tablespoon flour
- ½ teaspoon baking powder
- ½ teaspoon apple cider vinegar
- 1 tablespoon brown sugar
- 1 teaspoon ground cinnamon
- 1 egg
- 1 tablespoon margarine
- ¼ teaspoon nutmeg

Directions:

1. Beat the egg in the bowl and whisk it.
2. Melt the margarine and combine it together with the whisked egg.
3. Add nutmeg, apple cider vinegar, brown sugar, baking powder, and flour.
4. Knead the smooth and non-sticky dough.
5. Then make 4 bites from the dough.
6. Preheat the air fryer to 400 F.
7. Place the sweet bites on the air fryer rack and cook for 4 minutes.
8. Then flip the bites to another side and cook for 2 minutes more.
9. When the meal is cooked – serve it warm.
10. Enjoy!

Nutrition: calories 162, fat 8.1, fiber 1.1, carbs 18.2, protein 4.5

Salty Garlic Pretzels

Prep time: 20 minutes
Cooking time: 4 minutes
Servings: 2
Ingredients:

- 3 tablespoon boiling water
- 7 tablespoon flour
- 1 pinch dry yeast
- 1 pinch salt
- ½ tablespoon garlic powder
- 1 teaspoon olive oil
- ½ teaspoon sugar

Directions:

1. Combine together the dry yeast, salt, sugar, and garlic powder.
2. Shake the mixture and add flour.
3. After this, add the boiling water and knead the non-sticky dough.
4. Leave the dough in a warm place for 10 minutes.
5. Then roll the stick from the dough and cut it into 4 small logs.
6. Make the pretzels and brush them with the olive oil.
7. Preheat the air fryer to 360 F.
8. Put the pretzels in the air fryer basket and cook for 4 minutes.
9. When the pretzels are cooked – let them chill gently.
10. Enjoy!

Nutrition: calories 131, fat 2.6, fiber 1, carbs 23.5, protein 3.3

Cinnamon Apple Rings

Prep time: 10 minutes
Cooking time: 8 minutes
Servings: 2
Ingredients:

- 2 apples
- ½ teaspoon ground cinnamon
- 1 teaspoon brown sugar
- 1 teaspoon olive oil

Directions:

1. Wash the apples carefully and remove the seeds to make the holes in the apples.
2. Then slice the apples. You should get the shape of rings.
3. Preheat the air fryer to 360 F.
4. Place the apple rings in the air fryer basket and spray with the olive oil.
5. Cook for 8 minutes.
6. Shake the apple rings every 2 minutes.
7. Meanwhile, combine together the ground cinnamon and brown sugar. Shake the mixture.
8. When the apple rings are cooked – toss them in the sugar mixture and shake well.
9. Serve the apple rings and enjoy!

Nutrition: calories 143, fat 2.7, fiber 5.7, carbs 32.7, protein 0.6

Pepper Corn Fritters

Prep time: 10 minutes
Cooking time: 12 minutes
Servings: 2
Ingredients:

- 4 tablespoon flour
- 2 oz sweet corn kernels
- 1/3 teaspoon sugar
- 1 pinch salt
- ¼ teaspoon ground black pepper
- 1 tablespoon cream
- 1 egg
- ½ teaspoon olive oil

Directions:

1. Separate the egg yolk and egg white.
2. Whisk the egg yolk and combine together with the cream.
3. Add sugar, ground black pepper, and flour.
4. After this, add corn kernels and mix the mixture.
5. Whisk the egg white till the strong peaks.
6. Add the egg white to the dough and mix it up.
7. Preheat the air fryer to 370 F.
8. Spray the air fryer basket with the olive oil inside.
9. Then separate the dough into 2 servings.
10. Pour the first serving in the air fryer basket and cook for 3 minutes from each side.
11. Repeat the same steps with the second serving.
12. Serve the cooked fritters immediately.
13. Enjoy!

Nutrition: calories 237, fat 5.7, fiber 4.7, carbs 42.1, protein 9.5

Cheddar Hot Dogs

Prep time: 10 minutes
Cooking time: 9 minutes
Servings: 2
Ingredients:

- 2 hot dog buns
- 4 Cheddar cheese slices
- 2 pork sausages
- 2 teaspoon pesto sauce

Directions:

1. Preheat the air fryer to 375 F.
2. Put the sausages in the air fryer basket and cook for 8 minutes.
3. Meanwhile, spread the hot dog buns with the pesto sauce.
4. Then transfer the cooked sausages in the hot dog buns.
5. Place the cheese slices over the sausages.
6. Put the hot dogs in the air fryer basket and cook for 1 minute at 400 F.
7. Serve the cooked meal immediately.
8. Enjoy!

Nutrition: calories 480, fat 30.4, fiber 0.1, carbs 26.1, protein 22.7

Kale Chips

Prep time: 8 minutes
Cooking time: 4 minutes
Servings: 2
Ingredients:

- 7 oz kale
- 1 teaspoon dried oregano
- 1 teaspoon dried dill
- ¼ teaspoon salt
- 1 teaspoon garlic powder
- 1 tablespoon olive oil
- 1 teaspoon nutritional yeast

Directions:

1. Place the kale in the bowl.
2. Sprinkle it with the dried oregano, dried dill, salt, garlic powder, and nutritional yeast.
3. Mix the kale carefully and add olive oil.
4. Mix it carefully again.
5. Preheat the air fryer to 375 F.
6. Put the kale in the air fryer basket and cook for 4 minutes.
7. Shake the kale during cooking.
8. Chill the cooked kale and serve.
9. Enjoy!

Nutrition: calories 123, fat 7.2, fiber 2.4, carbs 12.9, protein 4.2

Coriander Shrimp Cakes

Prep time: 15 minutes
Cooking time: 6 minutes
Servings: 2
Ingredients:

- 6 oz shrimps, peeled
- 1 teaspoon ground coriander
- 2 tablespoon semolina
- 1 egg
- 1 tablespoon fresh parsley, chopped
- ¼ teaspoon chili flakes
- 1 teaspoon butter
- ½ teaspoon salt
- 1 tablespoon oatmeal flour

Directions:

1. Chop the peeled shrimps into the tiny pieces.
2. Crack the egg in the chopped shrimps.
3. Add semolina, chopped fresh parsley, ground coriander, chili flakes, salt, and oatmeal flour.
4. Mix the shrimp mixture carefully until homogenous.
5. Then preheat the air fryer to 400 F.
6. Melt the butter in the air fryer basket.
7. Make medium shrimp cakes and put them in the melted butter.
8. Cook the shrimp cakes for 3 minutes on each side.
9. When the shrimp cakes are cooked - chill them and serve.
10. Enjoy!

Nutrition: calories 188, fat 5.7, fiber 0.5, carbs 9.2, protein 23.5

Crunchy Avocado Sticks

Prep time: 15 minutes
Cooking time: 9 minutes
Servings: 2
Ingredients:

- 1 egg white
- 1/3 cup panko breadcrumbs
- 1 teaspoon olive oil
- 1 avocado, pitted
- ½ teaspoon salt
- ½ teaspoon ground black pepper

Directions:

1. Peel the avocado and cut it into the medium sticks.
2. Then whisk the egg white gently.
3. Place the avocado sticks in the egg white and stir well.
4. Then combine together panko bread crumbs, salt, and ground black pepper.
5. Coat the avocado sticks in the panko breadcrumbs.
6. Preheat the air fryer to 400 F.
7. Put the avocado sticks in the air fryer rack and spray them with the olive oil.
8. Cook the avocado sticks for 9 minutes.
9. Flip the avocado sticks in halfway of cooking.
10. Serve the avocado sticks warm.
11. Enjoy!

Nutrition: calories 306, fat 22.9, fiber 7.7, carbs 22.1, protein 6.2

Pickles in Paprika

Prep time: 10 minutes
Cooking time: 8 minutes
Servings: 2
Ingredients:

- 11 oz pickles
- 4 tablespoon flour
- ¼ teaspoon baking soda
- ½ teaspoon salt
- 1 tablespoon beer
- 2 tablespoon water
- 4 tablespoon panko breadcrumbs
- 1 teaspoon paprika

Directions:

1. Slice the pickles and dry them well.
2. Then combine together the flour, baking soda, salt, beer, and water.
3. Stir the mixture until homogenous.
4. Then dip the pickles slices in the flour mixture.
5. Combine the panko breadcrumbs and paprika in the separate bowl.
6. Then coat the pickles slices with the panko breadcrumbs.
7. Preheat the air fryer to 365 F.
8. Place the pickles onto the air fryer rack and cook for 8 minutes.
9. Flip the pickles after 5 minutes of cooking.
10. When the pickles are cooked – let them chill gently and serve.
11. Enjoy!

Nutrition: calories 105, fat 1.3, fiber 3.1, carbs 20.1, protein 3.3

Bacon Eggs

Prep time: 10 minutes
Cooking time: 10 minutes
Servings: 2
Ingredients:

- 4 eggs, boiled
- 4 bacon slices
- 1 teaspoon olive oil
- ½ teaspoon salt
- ½ teaspoon ground white pepper

Directions:

1. Peel the eggs.
2. Sprinkle the bacon slices with the olive oil, salt, and ground white pepper.
3. Then wrap the eggs in the bacon slices and secure every egg with 1 toothpick.
4. Preheat the air fryer to 380 F.
5. Put the bacon eggs in the air fryer basket and cook for 10 minutes.
6. Shake the eggs after 5 minutes of cooking.
7. When the meal is cooked – let it chill well.
8. Enjoy!

Nutrition: calories 353, fat 27, fiber 0.1, carbs 1.6, protein 25.2

Parmesan Zucchini Chips

Prep time: 10 minutes
Cooking time: 8 minutes
Servings: 2
Ingredients:

- 1 zucchini
- 3 oz Parmesan, shredded
- 1 tablespoon Italian seasoning
- 5 tablespoon panko breadcrumbs
- 1 tablespoon olive oil
- ½ teaspoon ground paprika
- 1 egg, beaten

Directions:

1. Slice the zucchini and dry the zucchini slices. The zucchini slices should be very thin.
2. Combine together panko breadcrumbs and Italian seasoning.
3. Add ground paprika and stir the mixture gently.
4. Whisk the egg.
5. Dip the zucchini slices in the whisked egg.
6. After this, coat the zucchini with the panko breadcrumbs.
7. Preheat the air fryer to 360 F.
8. Put the zucchini slices in the air fryer basket and cook for 7 minutes.
9. Shake the zucchini slices in halfway.
10. Sprinkle the chips with the shredded cheese and cook for 1 minute more.
11. Chill the zucchini chips and serve them.
12. Enjoy!

Nutrition: calories 311, fat 21, fiber 2.5, carbs 15.4, protein 19

Figs with Goat Cheese

Prep time: 10 minutes
Cooking time: 7 minutes
Servings: 2
Ingredients:

- 3 oz goat cheese
- 4 figs
- ½ teaspoon minced garlic
- 1 tablespoon olive oil
- 1 tablespoon fresh lemon juice
- ½ teaspoon ground ginger

Directions:

1. Make the cross cuts in the figs.
2. Remove ½ of all flesh from the figs.
3. Combine the minced garlic, olive oil, and ground ginger in the bowl.
4. Stir the mixture.
5. Add the goat cheese and stir it.
6. Then fill the figs with the goat cheese mixture well.
7. Preheat the air fryer to 360 F and put the figs in the air fryer basket.
8. Sprinkle the figs with the fresh lemon juice and cook for 7 minutes.
9. When the figs are cooked – serve them hot.
10. Enjoy!

Nutrition: calories 351, fat 22.6, fiber 3.8, carbs 25.9, protein 14.4

Paprika Chicken Bites

Prep time: 10 minutes
Cooking time: 8 minutes
Servings: 2
Ingredients:

- 4 tablespoon coconut flakes
- 3 tablespoon cream
- 1 tablespoon almond flour
- 1/3 teaspoon salt
- ½ teaspoon ground white pepper
- ½ teaspoon paprika
- 10 oz chicken fillet
- 1 teaspoon olive oil

Directions:

1. Combine together the cream, almond flour, salt, ground white pepper, and paprika.
2. Chop the chicken fillet into big bites.
3. Toss the chicken bites in the cream mixture.
4. Then coat the chicken bites with the coconut flakes.
5. Preheat the air fryer to 400 F.
6. Put the chicken bites in the air fryer basket and sprinkle with the olive oil.
7. Cook the chicken bites for 8 minutes.
8. Shake the chicken bites in halfway of cooking.
9. Chill the cooked meal and serve.
10. Enjoy!

Nutrition: calories 360, fat 18.9, fiber 1.6, carbs 3.5, protein 42.4

Celery Pork Balls

Prep time: 15 minutes
Cooking time: 11 minutes
Servings: 2
Ingredients:

- 1 tablespoon celery root
- 1 teaspoon minced garlic
- 1 oz carrot, grated
- 8 oz ground pork
- ½ teaspoon salt
- ¼ teaspoon ground nutmeg
- 1 teaspoon olive oil
- 1 tablespoon almond flour

Directions:

1. Combine together the celery root, minced garlic, grated carrot, ground pork, salt, ground nutmeg, and almond flour.
2. Mix the mixture until it is smooth.
3. After this, make the small balls from the forcemeat.
4. Preheat the air fryer to 390 F.
5. Place the ground pork balls in the air fryer basket and sprinkle them with the olive oil.
6. Cook the meatballs for 11 minutes.
7. When the meatballs are cooked – they will have little bit crunchy surface.
8. Enjoy the meal!

Nutrition: calories 215, fat 8.1, fiber 0.9, carbs 3.2, protein 30.7

Spinach Fritters

Prep time: 12 minutes
Cooking time: 8 minutes
Servings: 2
Ingredients:

- 4 oz spinach
- 1 tablespoon olive oil
- 1 egg
- 3 tablespoon semolina
- 2 tablespoon flour
- ½ teaspoon salt
- 3 oz ground chicken
- 3 tablespoon water
- 1 teaspoon turmeric

Directions:

1. Chop the spinach and put it in the bowl.
2. Beat the egg in the spinach.
3. Add semolina, flour, salt, ground chicken, and turmeric.
4. Add water and knead the fritters dough.
5. Preheat the air fryer to 376 F.
6. Make the medium fritters from the spinach mixture and place them in the air fryer.
7. Sprinkle the fritters with the olive oil and cook for 4 minutes from each side.
8. When the fritters are cooked – let them chill well.
9. Enjoy!

Nutrition: calories 274, fat 12.9, fiber 2.3, carbs 20.3, protein 19.6

Dill Radish Fries

Prep time: 10 minutes
Cooking time: 18 minutes
Servings: 2
Ingredients:

- 10 oz radish
- 1 teaspoon dried dill
- 1 teaspoon olive oil
- ½ teaspoon salt

Directions:

1. Wash the radish carefully and cut it into the halves.
2. Sprinkle the radish halves with the dried dill, olive oil, and salt.
3. Shake the radish well.
4. Preheat the air fryer to 370 F.
5. Put the radish in the air fryer and cook for 18 minutes.
6. Shake the radish 3 times during cooking.
7. When the radish fries are cooked – let them chill gently.
8. Enjoy!

Nutrition: calories 44, fat 2.5, fiber 2.3, carbs 5.1, protein 1.1

Beef Burgers

Prep time: 15 minutes
Cooking time: 16 minutes
Servings: 2
Ingredients:

- 4 tablespoon corn flakes crumbs
- 1 teaspoon ground paprika
- ¼ teaspoon ground ginger
- 1 teaspoon olive oil
- 8 oz minced beef
- ½ teaspoon onion powder
- ½ teaspoon garlic powder
- 1 egg
- ½ teaspoon salt

Directions:

1. Combine together the ground paprika, ground ginger, minced beef, onion powder, garlic powder, and salt.
2. Then beat the egg into the bowl and whisk it.
3. Make 2 medium burgers from the minced beef mixture.
4. Dip the beef burgers in the whisked egg.
5. Then sprinkle the burgers with the corn flakes crumbs.
6. Preheat the air fryer to 370 F.
7. Put the burgers in the air fryer and sprinkle them with the olive oil.
8. Cook the meal for 16 minutes.
9. Flip the burgers into another side after 8 minutes of cooking.
10. When the meal is cooked – enjoy it!

Nutrition: calories 270, fat 11.8, fiber 0.5, carbs 1.9, protein 37.5

Cilantro Eggplant Chips

Prep time: 10 minutes
Cooking time: 13 minutes
Servings: 2
Ingredients:

- 1 eggplants
- 1 tablespoon dried cilantro
- ½ tablespoon paprika
- 1 egg
- 1 teaspoon olive oil
- ½ teaspoon salt

Directions:

1. Wash the eggplant carefully and cut it into the chips.
2. Beat the egg in the bowl and whisk it.
3. Then sprinkle the eggplant chips with the whisked egg.
4. Sprinkle the eggplant with the dried cilantro, paprika, and salt.
5. Mix the eggplants carefully.
6. Preheat the air fryer to 400 F.
7. Place the eggplant chips in the air fryer basket and cook for 13 minutes. The time of cooking depends on the size of the chips.
8. Shake the chips after 5 minutes of cooking.
9. Chill the cooked chips and serve.
10. Enjoy!

Nutrition: calories 125, fat 5.2, fiber 10.3, carbs 17.3, protein 5.7

Chicken Mini Pies

Prep time: 15 minutes
Cooking time: 12 minutes
Servings: 2
Ingredients:

- ½ onion, sautéed
- 7 oz ground chicken
- 4 oz puff pastry
- 1 egg yolk
- ¼ teaspoon salt
- ¼ teaspoon ground white pepper
- 1 teaspoon olive oil

Directions:

1. Roll the puff pastry and cut it into 2 squares.
2. Whisk the egg yolk.
3. Combine together ground chicken, onion, salt, and ground white pepper.
4. Then put the ground chicken mixture in the center of puff pastry squares and secure them in the shape of pies.
5. Then brush the mini pies with the whisked egg yolk.
6. Preheat the air fryer to 370 F.
7. Spray the air fryer basket with olive oil inside.
8. Then place the pies in the air fryer and cook for 12 minutes.
9. When the pies are cooked – serve them and enjoy!

Nutrition: calories 560, fat 33.6, fiber 1.5, carbs 28.6, protein 34.5

Carrot & Potato Balls

Prep time: 10 minutes
Cooking time: 6 minutes
Servings: 2
Ingredients:

- 12 oz mashed potato
- 1 tablespoon fresh dill, chopped
- 1 oz carrot, grated
- 1 tablespoon flour
- 1 tablespoon butter
- ½ teaspoon salt

Directions:

1. Combine together mashed potato, chopped fresh dill, grated carrot, and flour.
2. Add salt and mix the mixture well.
3. Then make the medium balls from the potato mixture.
4. Preheat the air fryer to 400 F.
5. Toss the butter in the air fryer basket and melt it.
6. Add the potato balls in the air fryer basket and cook for 6 minutes.
7. Stir the potato balls after 3 minutes of cooking. The potato balls should have light brown color.
8. Serve the potato balls.
9. Enjoy!

Nutrition: calories 267, fat 13, fiber 3.2, carbs 34, protein 4.2

Parmesan Chicken Sticks

Prep time: 10 minutes
Cooking time: 11 minutes
Servings: 2
Ingredients:

- 8 oz chicken fillet
- ½ teaspoon salt
- 1 teaspoon curry paste
- 1 tablespoon cream
- 1 teaspoon oil
- 3 oz Parmesan, shredded

Directions:

1. Slice the chicken into the thick slices.
2. Then combine curry paste and cream together.
3. Whisk it and salt.
4. Then sprinkle the chicken slices with the curry mixture.
5. Preheat the air fryer to 400 F.
6. Put the chicken slices in the air fryer basket and sprinkle with the olive oil.
7. Cook the chicken for 9 minutes,
8. After this, sprinkle the chicken with the shredded cheese and cook for 2 minutes more.
9. When the chicken is cooked – let it chill gently.
10. Enjoy!

Nutrition: calories 393, fat 21.6, fiber 0, carbs 2.4, protein 46.7

Turmeric Carrot Balls

Prep time: 10 minutes
Cooking time: 4 minutes
Servings: 2
Ingredients:

- 2 carrot, boiled
- ½ teaspoon salt
- 1 tablespoon turmeric
- 1 tablespoon dried oregano
- 1 egg white
- 2 tablespoon flour
- 1 teaspoon olive oil
- 3 tablespoon plain yogurt

Directions:

1. Grate the carrot and combine it together with the salt, turmeric, dried oregano, egg white, flour, and plain yogurt.
2. Form the small balls from the carrot mixture.
3. Preheat the air fryer to 400 F.
4. Place the carrot balls in the air fryer and sprinkle them with the olive oil.
5. Cook the carrot balls for 4 minutes.
6. When the meal is cooked – chill it till the room temperature.
7. Enjoy!

Nutrition: calories 117, fat 3.3, fiber 3.4, carbs 17.4, protein 4.9

Corn Apple Tots

Prep time: 15 minutes
Cooking time: 6 minutes
Servings: 2
Ingredients:

- 1 egg
- 2 tablespoon cream
- 1 tablespoon sugar
- 1 tablespoon flour
- 1 teaspoon cornstarch
- 1 teaspoon olive oil

Directions:

1. Cut the apple into the big cubes.
2. Beat the egg in the bowl and whisk it.
3. Add the cream and sugar in the whisked egg.
4. After this, add flour and cornstarch.
5. Whisk the mixture until homogenous.
6. Preheat the air fryer to 370 F.
7. Spray the air fryer basket with the olive oil inside.
8. Then dip the apple cubes in the cream mixture.
9. Transfer the dipped apples to the air fryer.
10. Cook the apple tots for 6 minutes.
11. Shake the apples after 3 minutes of cooking.
12. When the apple tots have light brown color – they are cooked.
13. Enjoy!

Nutrition: calories 101, fat 5.2, fiber 0.1, carbs 10.7, protein 3.3

Sesame Pork Cubes

Prep time: 20 minutes
Cooking time: 10 minutes
Servings: 2
Ingredients:

- 1 tablespoon soy sauce
- 1 teaspoon sesame seeds, roasted
- 1 teaspoon paprika
- ½ teaspoon sugar
- 8 oz pork chops
- 1 tablespoon sesame oil
- ¼ teaspoon dried rosemary

Directions:

1. Cut the pork chops into the cubes.
2. Sprinkle the pork cubes with the paprika, sugar, soy sauce, dried rosemary, and sesame oil.
3. Mix the meat carefully.
4. After this, leave the meat for 10 minutes to marinate.
5. Preheat the air fryer to 400 F.
6. Put the marinated meat in the air fryer basket.
7. Add all the remaining liquid and cook the meat for 10 minutes.
8. Stir the meat after 6 minutes of cooking.
9. Sprinkle the pork cubes with the sesame seeds and stir the meat gently one more time.
10. Serve the meal immediately.
11. Enjoy!

Nutrition: calories 443, fat 35.9, fiber 0.7, carbs 2.7, protein 26.4

Parmesan Egg Clouds

Prep time: 8 minutes
Cooking time: 4 minutes
Servings: 2
Ingredients:

- 2 egg whites
- ¼ teaspoon olive oil
- ¼ teaspoon salt
- 1 oz Parmesan, shredded

Directions:

1. Pour the egg whites into the bowl and mix them with the help of the hand mixer for 3 minutes or till you get the stiff peaks.
2. Add salt and stir gently.
3. Preheat the air fryer to 400 F.
4. Spray the air fryer basket with the olive oil inside.
5. Then make the medium clouds from the egg whites and place them in the air fryer basket.
6. Cook the egg whites clouds for 3 minutes.
7. Then sprinkle the meal with the shredded cheese and cook for 1 minute more.
8. When the egg whites clouds are cooked – chill them till the room temperature and serve.
9. Enjoy!

Nutrition: calories 68, fat 3.7, fiber 0, carbs 0.8, protein 8.2

Bacon Mozzarella

Prep time: 10 minutes
Cooking time: 9 minutes
Servings: 2
Ingredients:

- 4 Mozzarella balls
- 4 slices of bacon
- 1 teaspoon olive oil
- 1 teaspoon dried oregano
- ¼ teaspoon ground paprika

Directions:

1. Sprinkle the bacon slices with the dried oregano and ground paprika.
2. Wrap Mozzarella balls in the bacon slices and secure with toothpicks.
3. Sprinkle Mozzarella balls with the olive oil.
4. Preheat the air fryer to 375 F and put the balls in the air fryer basket.
5. Cook the snack for 9 minutes.
6. Shake the snack gently after 4 minutes of cooking.
7. Then let the cooked meal chill gently.
8. Enjoy!

Nutrition: calories 507, fat 38.8, fiber 0.4, carbs 2, protein 33.5

Creamy Salmon Pieces

Prep time: 10 minutes
Cooking time: 10 minutes
Servings: 2
Ingredients:

- 2 tablespoon cream
- 1 tablespoon flour
- ¼ cup panko breadcrumbs
- ¼ teaspoon chili flakes
- ¼ teaspoon salt
- 8 oz salmon fillet
- 1 teaspoon olive oil

Directions:

1. Combine together flour and cream.
2. Mix the mixture.
3. Then cut the salmon fillet into 2 pieces.
4. Sprinkle the salmon pieces with the chili flakes and salt.
5. Dip the salmon fillets in the flour mixture.
6. Then coat the salmon pieces in the panko breadcrumbs.
7. Preheat the air fryer to 380 F.
8. Spray the salmon pieces with the olive oil and put in the air fryer basket.
9. Cook the fish for 10 minutes.
10. When the fish pieces are cooked – chill them little and serve.
11. Enjoy!

Nutrition: calories 227, fat 10.3, fiber 1.1, carbs 10.9, protein 23.5

Hot Beet Chips

Prep time: 10 minutes
Cooking time: 12 minutes
Servings: 2
Ingredients:

- 7 oz beets
- 1 teaspoon chili flakes
- ½ teaspoon red pepper
- 1 teaspoon olive oil
- ¼ teaspoon sage

Directions:

1. Wash the beet carefully and slice into the chips.
2. Sprinkle the beet chips with the chili flakes, red pepper, olive oil, and sage.
3. Mix up the beet chips carefully.
4. Preheat the air fryer to 360 F.
5. Put the beet chips in the air fryer basket in one layer and cook for 10 minutes.
6. Then shake the chips gently and cook for 2 minutes more.
7. When the beet chips are cooked – let them chill till the room temperature and serve.
8. Enjoy!

Nutrition: calories 74, fat 2.6, fiber 2.4, carbs 12.2, protein 2

Desserts

Sweet Pumpkin Loaf

Prep time: 20 minutes
Cooking time: 20 minutes
Servings: 2
Ingredients:

- ½ teaspoon baking soda
- 2 tablespoon pumpkin seeds
- 1 egg
- ¼ cup milk
- 1/3 cup flour
- 2 tablespoon brown sugar
- 1 teaspoon vanilla extract
- ½ teaspoon olive oil
- 1 teaspoon fresh lemon juice
- 1 teaspoon lime zest
- 1 pinch salt

Directions:

1. Combine together baking soda, flour, brown sugar, vanilla extract, fresh lemon juice, lime zest, and salt in the bowl.
2. Beat the egg in the flour mixture.
3. Add milk and stir the mixture gently with the help of the fork.
4. Crush the pumpkin seeds gently and put them in the flour mixture.
5. Then knead the soft and elastic dough. Add more flour if desired.
6. Let the dough rest for 10 minutes.
7. Preheat the air fryer to 350 F.
8. Spray the loaf tin with the olive oil and put the dough there.
9. Cook the pumpkin seeds loaf for 15 minutes.
10. After this, reduce the temperature to 320 F and cook the loaf for 5 minutes more.
11. Check if the meal is cooked – and transfer it to the serving plate.
12. Slice the sweet pumpkin seeds loaf.
13. Enjoy!

Nutrition: calories 221, fat 8.2, fiber 1, carbs 28.4, protein 8.1

Milky Egg Custard

Prep time: 15 minutes
Cooking time: 20 minutes
Servings: 2
Ingredients:

- 1 egg yolk
- ¼ cup milk
- ½ teaspoon potato starch
- 1 teaspoon white sugar
- ¼ teaspoon vanilla extract

Directions:

1. Preheat the air fryer to 210 F.
2. Preheat the milk until it starts to boil.
3. Then whisk together the egg yolk and white sugar.
4. Pour the egg yolk mixture into the hot milk slowly. Whisk it constantly.
5. Add vanilla extract and potato starch. Whisk it well until the mixture is homogenous.
6. Pour the egg mixture into 2 ramekins.
7. Place the ramekins in the air fryer basket.
8. Cook the egg custard for 20 minutes.
9. When the dessert is cooked – let it chill to the room temperature.
10. Enjoy!

Nutrition: calories 55, fat 2.9, fiber 0, carbs 4.9, protein 2.4

Raisins Carrot Pie

Prep time: 20 minutes
Cooking time: 35 minutes
Servings: 2
Ingredients:

- 3 tablespoon flour
- 2 oz carrot, grated
- 1 tablespoon raisins
- ¼ teaspoon baking soda
- ½ teaspoon apple cider vinegar
- ¼ teaspoon ground cinnamon
- 1 pinch salt
- 2 teaspoon brown sugar
- 1 egg
- 2 tablespoon milk

Directions:

1. Sift the flour into the bowl.
2. Add grated carrot, raisins, baking soda, apple cider vinegar, ground cinnamon, salt, brown sugar, and milk.
3. Stir the mixture gently.
4. Beat the egg in the separate bowl and whisk it.
5. Pour the whisked egg into the flour mixture.
6. Mix it up until homogenous. The mixture should look like a thick batter.
7. Preheat the air fryer to 350 F.
8. Cover the air fryer tray with the parchment and pour the dough there.
9. Cover the dough with the foil.
10. Pin the foil to give the dough the opportunity to "breath".
11. Put the pie in the air fryer and cook for 35 minutes.
12. Then discard the foil and cook the pie for 2 minutes more at 400 F.
13. When the pie is cooked – chill it till the room temperature.
14. Serve!

Nutrition: calories 119, fat 2.6, fiber 1.3, carbs 19.4, protein 4.9

Cracker Cheesecake

Prep time: 15 minutes
Cooking time: 17 minutes
Servings: 2
Ingredients:

- 1 teaspoon butter
- 3 oz graham crackers
- 3 oz cream cheese
- 1 tablespoon brown sugar
- 1 egg
- ¼ teaspoon vanilla extract

Directions:

1. Preheat the air fryer to 360 F.
2. Crush the graham crackers and combine them with the butter.
3. Then cover the air fryer tray with the parchment and put the cracker mixture.
4. Press it gently and slide the tray into the air fryer.
5. Cook the cheesecake crust for 2 minutes.
6. Then beat the egg in the cream cheese.
7. Add brown sugar and vanilla extract.
8. Mix the mixture carefully until smooth.
9. Pour the cream cheese mixture over the cheesecake crust and flatten it with the help of the spatula.
10. Reduce the air fryer temperature to 310 F.
11. Put the cheesecake in the air fryer and cook for 15 minutes.
12. After this, chill the cheesecake well.
13. Serve it!

Nutrition: calories 109, fat 8.8, fiber 0.8, carbs 3.8, protein 5.2

Ginger Apricot Tart

Prep time: 15 minutes
Cooking time: 10 minutes
Servings: 2
Ingredients:

- 2 tablespoon butter
- 4 tablespoons flour
- 1 pinch salt
- 2 teaspoon sugar
- 2 big apricots
- 1 teaspoon butter
- ¼ teaspoon ground ginger

Directions:

1. Combine together the butter, flour, and salt in the mixing bowl.
2. Knead the soft, elastic dough.
3. Roll the dough and separate it into 2 parts.
4. Make the rounds from the dough with the help of the cutter.
5. Then halve the apricots and remove the stones from them.
6. Slice the apricots.
7. Place the apricots in the center of the dough.
8. Roll the edges of the tarts.
9. Add ½ teaspoon of butter on the top of every tart.
10. Then sprinkle the tarts with the ground ginger and sugar.
11. Preheat the air fryer to 360 F.
12. Place the apricot tarts there and cook for 10 minutes.
13. Chill the cooked tarts till the room temperature.
14. Enjoy!

Nutrition: calories 217, fat 14.8, fiber 1.1, carbs 19.9, protein 2.2

Banana Oatmeal Bites

Prep time: 10 minutes
Cooking time: 8 minutes
Servings: 2
Ingredients:

- 2 bananas
- 1 egg white
- 1 teaspoon coconut sugar
- 1 tablespoon oatmeal flour
- 2 tablespoon panko breadcrumbs
- 1 teaspoon ground cinnamon
- ¼ teaspoon ground nutmeg

Directions:

1. Peel the bananas and cut them into the bites.
2. Combine together coconut sugar, panko bread crumbs, ground cinnamon, and ground nutmeg.
3. Then whisk the egg white gently.
4. Coat the banana bites with the oatmeal flour.
5. Then dip them in the whisked egg white.
6. After this, coat the banana bites with the coconut sugar mixture.
7. Place the banana bites in the air fryer basket.
8. Cook the banana bites at 360 F for 8 minutes.
9. Let the cooked dessert chill briefly.
10. Enjoy!

Nutrition: calories 159, fat 1.1, fiber 4.3, carbs 35.7, protein 4.5

Honey Pumpkin Delights

Prep time: 20 minutes
Cooking time: 7 minutes
Servings: 2
Ingredients:

- ¼ teaspoon ground anise
- ¼ teaspoon vanilla extract
- 2 teaspoon honey
- ¼ teaspoon ground cinnamon
- ½ teaspoon ground ginger
- 1 teaspoon butter
- 10 oz pumpkin

Directions:

1. Peel the pumpkin and cut it into 4 pieces.
2. Combine together vanilla extract, ground anise, honey, ground cinnamon, ground ginger, and butter,
3. Churn the mixture. Preheat it if desired.
4. Then sprinkle the pumpkin pieces with the spice mixture and leave them for 15 minutes or till the pumpkin gives the juice.
5. Then preheat the air fryer to 400 F.
6. Put the pumpkin pieces in the air fryer basket.
7. Sprinkle the pumpkin pieces with the remaining juice mixture.
8. Cook the pumpkin pieces for 7 minutes.
9. Shake the pumpkin pieces after 3 minutes of cooking.
10. When the pumpkin pieces are cooked – they should be tender.
11. Let the cooked pumpkin pieces cool briefly.
12. Serve the dessert immediately or keep it in the fridge.
13. Enjoy!

Nutrition: calories 91, fat 2.4, fiber 4.4, carbs 18, protein 1.7

Nutmeg Blueberry Crumble

Prep time: 15 minutes
Cooking time: 15 minutes
Servings: 2
Ingredients:

- 3 tablespoon blueberry
- 1 tablespoon brown sugar
- 1 teaspoon lemon juice
- ¼ teaspoon ground nutmeg
- 2 tablespoon butter, soft
- 4 tablespoons flour
- ¼ teaspoon olive oil
- 2 teaspoon white sugar

Directions:

1. Mash the blueberries with the help of the fork.
2. Add lemon juice and brown sugar.
3. Mix the mixture up and add ground nutmeg.
4. Then combine together flour, soft butter, and white sugar.
5. Knead the soft dough.
6. Crumble the dough with the help of the fingertips.
7. Separate the crumbled dough into 2 parts.
8. Then cover the cake tin with the parchment.
9. Place the first part of the crumbled dough in the cake tin,
10. After this, spread the blueberry mixture over the dough.
11. Sprinkle the blueberry mixture with the second part of the dough.
12. Preheat the air fryer to 360 F.
13. Put the crumble in the air fryer and cook for 15 minutes.
14. When the dessert is cooked – let it chill briefly.
15. Enjoy!

Nutrition: calories 206, fat 12.4, fiber 0.8, carbs 22.5, protein 1.9

Cherry Crust Pie

Prep time: 15 minutes
Cooking time: 10 minutes
Servings: 2
Ingredients:

- 6 oz pie crust, uncooked
- 2 oz cherry, pitted
- 1 teaspoon brown sugar
- 1 teaspoon water
- ¼ teaspoon turmeric

Directions:

1. Roll the pie crust and place the cherries there.
2. Sprinkle the cherries with the brown sugar and turmeric.
3. Place the pie in the air fryer basket and sprinkle the edges of the pie with water.
4. Preheat the air fryer to 360 F.
5. Cook the pie for 10 minutes.
6. Then chill the cherry pie to the room temperature.
7. Enjoy!

Nutrition: calories 157, fat 5, fiber 2.6, carbs 28, protein 2.6

Cream Cheesecake Soufflé

Prep time: 15 minutes
Cooking time: 10 minutes
Servings: 2
Ingredients:

- 5 oz cream cheese
- 1 egg yolk
- 1 egg
- 1 teaspoon butter
- 2 tablespoons brown sugar
- ½ teaspoon vanilla extract
- ½ teaspoon almond flakes

Directions:

1. Beat the egg in the bowl.
2. Add the egg yolk and brown sugar.
3. Mix the mixture with the help of the hand mixer.
4. Then add butter, cream cheese, and vanilla extract.
5. Mix the mixture with the help of the hand mixer for 2 minutes at the maximum speed.
6. After this, pour the cream cheese mixture into 2 ramekins.
7. Preheat the air fryer to 350 F.
8. Place the ramekins in the air fryer basket and cook for 10 minutes.
9. The soufflé is cooked when you get the light brown color of the surface.
10. Let the soufflé chill for 5 minutes.
11. Then sprinkle the soufflé with the almond flakes.
12. Enjoy!

Nutrition: calories 363, fat 31.3, fiber 0.1, carbs 11.4, protein 9.6

Creamy Chocolate Profiteroles

Prep time: 15 minutes
Cooking time: 10 minutes
Servings: 2
Ingredients:

- 3 tablespoons flour
- 1 tablespoon butter
- 1 egg
- 2 tablespoon water
- 2 tablespoon whipped cream

Directions:

1. Boil the water and melt the butter.
2. Combine together boiled water, butter, and flour.
3. Mix the mixture and beat the egg.
4. Then mix the dough with the help of the mixer.
5. When you get the plastic dough – transfer it to the pastry bag.
6. Preheat the air fryer to 360 F.
7. Make the profiteroles with the help of the special nozzle and transfer them in the air fryer basket.
8. Cook the profiteroles for 10 minutes,
9. Then chill the profiteroles and cut them crosswise.
10. Fill the profiteroles with the whipped cream.
11. Enjoy!

Nutrition: calories 338, fat 25.4, fiber 0.6, carbs 19.1, protein 8 .7

Oats Cookies

Prep time: 10 minutes
Cooking time: 9 minutes
Servings: 2
Ingredients:

- 3 tablespoon oatmeal flour
- 2 tablespoon sour cream
- 1 tablespoon brown sugar
- 1 teaspoon butter
- 1 pinch salt
- ½ teaspoon ground cardamom
- 1 egg

Directions:

1. Beat the egg in the bowl and whisk it.
2. Add the oatmeal flour and flour in the whisked egg.
3. After this, add sour cream, brown sugar, butter, salt, and ground cardamom.
4. Mix the mixture to get the homogenous dough.
5. Preheat the air fryer to 360 F.
6. Cover the air fryer basket with the parchment.
7. Make the medium cookies from the dough. Use the spoon for this step.
8. Place the cookies in the air fryer basket and cook for 9 minutes.
9. When the cookies are cooked – chill them well.
10. Taste and enjoy!

Nutrition: calories 115, fat 7, fiber 0.8, carbs 9.3, protein 4.2

Chocolate Butter Balls

Prep time: 10 minutes
Cooking time: 10 minutes
Servings: 2
Ingredients:

- 1 tablespoon chocolate chips
- 1 tablespoon butter
- 3 tablespoon flour
- 1 tablespoon cocoa powder
- ¼ teaspoon vanilla extract

Directions:

1. Melt the chocolate chips and butter.
2. Combine together the melted ingredients.
3. Then add flour and vanilla extract.
4. Mix the mixture and knead the smooth dough.
5. Make the medium balls from the chocolate mixture.
6. Preheat the air fryer to 360 F.
7. Place the chocolate balls in the air fryer basket and cook for 5 minutes.
8. After this, reduce the temperature to 345 F and cook the dessert for 5 minutes more.
9. When the chocolate balls are cooked – sprinkle them with the cocoa powder.
10. Serve the dessert and enjoy!

Nutrition: calories 129, fat 7.8, fiber 1.3, carbs 13.6, protein 2.2

Apricot Cinnamon Crumble

Prep time: 15 minutes
Cooking time: 20 minutes
Servings: 2
Ingredients:

- ¼ cup fresh apricot
- 1 tablespoon brown sugar
- 1 tablespoon butter
- ½ teaspoon ground cinnamon
- 3 tablespoon flour
- 1 teaspoon lime juice

Directions:

1. Halve the apricots and then remove the stones.
2. Then chop the apricots and sprinkle with the ½ tablespoon of sugar.
3. Sprinkle the apricots with the lemon juice.
4. Mix the mixture.
5. Then combine together butter, remaining brown sugar, ground cinnamon, and flour.
6. Knead the dough.
7. Then crumble the dough with the help of the fingertips.
8. Put the apricot mixture into the cake tin and spread it well.
9. Then sprinkle the apricots with the crumbled dough.
10. Press it gently.
11. Preheat the air fryer to 360 F.
12. Put the cake tin in the air fryer and cook for 20 minutes.
13. When the meal is cooked – let it chill briefly.
14. Enjoy!

Nutrition: calories 121, fat 6, fiber 1, carbs 16, protein 1.6

Cinnamon Doughnuts

Prep time: 15 minutes
Cooking time: 15 minutes
Servings: 2
Ingredients:

- 1 teaspoon sugar
- 1 teaspoon butter
- 1/3 cup flour
- ¼ teaspoon salt
- 1 egg yolk
- 3 tablespoon sour cream
- 1 teaspoon ground cinnamon
- 1 tablespoon brown sugar

Directions:

1. Combine together brown sugar, butter, flour, salt, and sour cream.
2. Knead the smooth and non-sticky dough.
3. Then roll the dough using the rolling pin.
4. After this, use the cutter to make the medium doughnuts.
5. Whisk the egg yolk.
6. Preheat the air fryer to 360 F.
7. Brush the doughnuts with the whisked egg and put in the air fryer.
8. Cook the doughnuts for 15 minutes.
9. When the surface of the doughnuts is light brown – flip them to another side.
10. Meanwhile, combine together sugar with the cinnamon.
11. When the doughnuts are cooked – sprinkle them gently with the sugar-cinnamon mixture.
12. Serve the doughnuts immediately.
13. Enjoy!

Nutrition: calories 186, fat 8.2, fiber 1.2, carbs 24.3, protein 4.2

Raisin Vanilla Muffins

Prep time: 15 minutes
Cooking time: 10 minutes
Servings: 2
Ingredients:

- 1 oz raisins
- ¼ cup flour
- 2 tablespoon butter
- ¼ teaspoon baking soda
- 1 tablespoon brown sugar
- 1 egg
- ½ teaspoon vanilla extract
- 1 teaspoon apple cider vinegar

Directions:

1. Preheat the air fryer to 360 F.
2. Combine together flour, baking soda, and brown sugar.
3. Then add raisins, butter, vanilla extract, and apple cider vinegar.
4. Crack the egg into the mixture.
5. Take the fork and mix the mixture well.
6. Then use the hand mixer to make the homogenous mass. The dough should be liquid as a batter.
7. Pour the muffin dough into the muffin molds.
8. Place the muffin molds in the air fryer basket.
9. Cook the muffins for 10 minutes or until the top of the muffins are light brown.
10. When the raisin muffins are cooked – let them chill little.
11. Then discard the muffins from the muffin molds (if you use the silicone molds).
12. Enjoy!

Nutrition: calories 253, fat 13.9, fiber 0.9, carbs 27.9, protein 5

Chocolate Chip Muffins

Prep time: 15 minutes
Cooking time: 10 minutes
Servings: 2
Ingredients:

- 2 oz chocolate chips
- 2 oz butter
- 1 egg
- 1 teaspoon vanilla extract
- 1 teaspoon sour cream
- 1 teaspoon cocoa powder
- 1/3 cup flour
- 1 tablespoon sugar
- 1 teaspoon lemon juice

Directions:

1. Make the butter soft and combine it with the vanilla extract and sour cream.
2. Add cocoa powder, flour, sugar, and lemon juice.
3. After this beat the egg in the flour mixture and mix it with the help of the hand mixer until homogenous.
4. Sprinkle the dough with the chocolate chips and stir it carefully.
5. Preheat the air fryer to 365 F.
6. Use the spoon to fill the muffin molds with the dough.
7. Put the muffin molds in the air fryer basket.
8. Cook the muffins for 10 minutes.
9. Then check if the muffins are cooked using the toothpick.
10. Chill the muffins till the room temperature.
11. Serve the dessert!

Nutrition: calories 498, fat 34.4, fiber 1.8, carbs 39.8, protein 7.6

Cocoa Brownies

Prep time: 15 minutes
Cooking time: 15 minutes
Servings: 2
Ingredients:

- 3 tablespoon cocoa powder
- 1 tablespoon nuts, crushed
- 1 pinch salt
- 1 egg
- 3 tablespoon flour
- 4 tablespoon butter, soft
- 2 tablespoon brown sugar

Directions:

1. Beat the egg in the mixing bowl and whisk it.
2. Combine the cocoa powder, salt, flour, and brown sugar in the separate bowl.
3. Stir the mixture.
4. Put the dried mixture in the mixing bowl.
5. Add crushed nuts.
6. Melt the butter and pour it into the mixture.
7. Mix it up to make the smooth dough.
8. Preheat the air fryer to 350 F.
9. Pour the brownie dough into the air fryer tray and flatten it gently with the help of the spatula.
10. Cook the brownie for 15 minutes.
11. Check if the brownie is cooked and remove it from the air fryer.
12. Place the brownie on the chopping plate.
13. Cut it into the serving pieces.
14. Enjoy!

Nutrition: calories 355, fat 28.6, fiber 3.1, carbs 23.5, protein 6.4

Walnut Baked Apples

Prep time: 15 minutes
Cooking time: 20
Servings: 2
Ingredients:

- 2 apples
- 2 teaspoon walnuts, crushed
- 2 teaspoon ground cinnamon
- 2 teaspoon brown sugar
- 1 teaspoon ground ginger
- 2 teaspoon butter
- 2 teaspoon honey
- 1 teaspoon vanilla extract

Directions:

1. Make the small holes in the apples and remove the seeds.
2. Combine the crushed walnuts, ground cinnamon, brown sugar, ground ginger, butter, honey, and vanilla extract.
3. Mix the mixture carefully.
4. Then fill the apple holes with the walnut mixture.
5. Preheat the air fryer to 350 F.
6. Put the apples in the air fryer basket and cook 20 minutes.
7. When the apples are baked – chill them for 3 minutes.
8. Transfer the baked eggs to the serving plates.
9. Enjoy!

Nutrition: calories 213, fat 5.8, fiber 6.9, carbs 42.5, protein 1.

Nutmeg Apricot Muffins

Prep time: 15 minutes
Cooking time: 12 minutes
Servings: 2
Ingredients:

- 1 tablespoon apricot jam
- 2 apricots
- ½ teaspoon ground nutmeg
- 1 teaspoon lemon juice
- 5 tablespoon flour
- 3 tablespoon butter
- ½ teaspoon baking soda
- 1 teaspoon vanilla extract
- 3 tablespoon brown sugar

Directions:

1. Halve the apricots and remove the stones.
2. Chop the apricots and combine them with the jam.
3. Add brown sugar, lemon juice, ground nutmeg, baking soda, and vanilla extract.
4. Mix the mixture up and add flour.
5. Then melt the butter and add it to the ham mixture.
6. Use the hand mixer to make the homogenous dough.
7. Preheat the air fryer to 360 F.
8. Fill ½ part of every muffin mold with the dough and place them in the air fryer basket.
9. Cook the muffins for 12 minutes.
10. When the muffins are cooked – let them chill briefly and remove from the air fryer basket.
11. Serve the muffins and enjoy!

Nutrition: calories 326, fat 17.9, fiber 1.4, carbs 39, protein 2.8

Cake with Vanilla Frosting

Prep time: 20 minutes
Cooking time: 25 minutes
Servings: 2
Ingredients:

- ¼ cup flour
- 2 tablespoon butter
- 1 egg
- ½ teaspoon vanilla extract
- ¼ cup sugar
- 4 tablespoon heavy cream
- 2 tablespoon brown sugar

Directions:

1. Separate the egg yolk and egg white.
2. Whisk the egg yolks with the sugar until you get the lemon color mixture.
3. Then add butter and flour.
4. Whisk the egg white until the strong peaks.
5. Then add the egg white to the egg yolk mixture.
6. Stir it carefully with the help of the spatula.
7. Preheat the air fryer to 360 F.
8. Transfer the dough to the air fryer cake tin and slice it in the air fryer.
9. Cook the sponge cake for 15 minutes.
10. After this, reduce the air fryer temperature to 350 F and cook the cake for 10 minutes more.
11. Meanwhile, make the frosting: whisk together brown sugar and heavy cream.
12. When the sponge cake is cooked – transfer it to the serving plate and spread with the frosting.
13. Serve the dessert and enjoy!

Nutrition: calories 425, fat 25, fiber 0.4, carbs 46.9, protein 5.1

Marshmallow & Butter Bananas

Prep time: 10 minutes
Cooking time: 5 minutes
Servings: 2
Ingredients:

- 2 bananas
- 2 tablespoon mini marshmallow
- 2 teaspoon peanut butter
- ¼ teaspoon ground cinnamon

Directions:

1. Do not peel the bananas and make the crosswise cuts in them.
2. Open the cuts of the bananas to make the pockets.
3. Sprinkle the banana pockets with the ground cinnamon.
4. Then add peanut butter and mini marshmallow.
5. Preheat the air fryer to 400 F.
6. Put the bananas in the air fryer basket and cook for 5 minutes or until the marshmallow starts to melt and the bananas are soft.
7. Transfer the cooked bananas to the serving plates and serve immediately.
8. Enjoy!

Nutrition: calories 183, fat 3.1, fiber 3.6, carbs 39.4, protein 2.7

Chocolate Sauce

Prep time: 8 minutes
Cooking time: 4 minutes
Servings: 2
Ingredients:

- 3 tablespoon chocolate chips
- 2 tablespoon heavy cream
- 1 teaspoon butter
- 1 tablespoon milk
- ½ teaspoon vanilla extract

Directions:

1. Melt the butter and combine it with the heavy cream and milk.
2. Add vanilla extract and mix the mixture.
3. Preheat the air fryer to 400 F.
4. Put the chocolate chips in the air fryer basket and cook them for 2 minutes.
5. When the chocolate chips are melted – add the heavy cream mixture.
6. Cook the mixture for 2 minutes more.
7. After this, stir the mixture with the help of the spatula and cook it for 2 minutes more.
8. Stir it carefully until the sauce is homogenous.
9. Pour the sauce into the ramekins and serve.
10. Enjoy!

Nutrition: calories 160, fat 12.3, fiber 0.5, carbs 10.3, protein 1.8

Apple Pastries

Prep time: 15 minutes
Cooking time: 8 minutes
Servings: 2
Ingredients:

- 1 red apples
- 2 teaspoon brown sugar
- 1 teaspoon ground cinnamon
- 2 teaspoon butter
- 3 oz puff pastry
- 1 egg yolk

Directions:

1. Roll the puff pastry and cut it into 2 squares.
2. Roll the edges of the squares.
3. Then halve the apple and slice it.
4. Place the apple slices in the center of dough squares.
5. Then sprinkle the apples with the ground cinnamon, sugar, and butter.
6. Whisk the egg yolk and brush the dough edges.
7. Preheat the air fryer to 400 F.
8. Cover the air fryer basket with the parchment and put the pastries there.
9. Cook the dessert for 8 minutes or until it is cooked.
10. Serve the cooked dessert immediately.
11. Enjoy!

Nutrition: calories 367, fat 22.5, fiber 4, carbs 38.8, protein 4.8

Cashew Cookies

Prep time: 15 minutes
Cooking time: 15 minutes
Servings: 2
Ingredients:

- 3 tablespoon flour
- 1 teaspoon butter
- 1 teaspoon cashew, crushed
- ½ teaspoon vanilla extract
- 1 tablespoon brown sugar
- ½ teaspoon cream

Directions:

1. Make the butter soft and place it in the big bowl.
2. Add flour and vanilla extract.
3. After this, add brown sugar and cream.
4. Knead the smooth and non-sticky dough.
5. Roll the dough and make the cookies with the help of the cutter.
6. Sprinkle every cookie with the crushed cashews.
7. Press the surface of the cookies lightly.
8. Preheat the air fryer to 360 F.
9. Put the cookies in the air fryer basket tray and cook the cookies for 15 minutes.
10. When the cookies are cooked – let them chill briefly.
11. Enjoy!

Nutrition: calories 88, fat 2.7, fiber 0.4, carbs 14, protein 1.5

Vanilla Oat Rolls

Prep time: 15 minutes
Cooking time: 17 minutes
Servings: 2
Ingredients:

- ¼ teaspoon active yeast
- 3 teaspoon brown sugar
- 1 teaspoon vanilla sugar
- 1 teaspoon vanilla extract
- 2 teaspoon butter
- 4 tablespoon flour
- 1 teaspoon oatmeal flour
- 1 pinch salt
- ½ teaspoon olive oil
- 2 tablespoon cream

Directions:

1. Preheat the cream to the room temperature and combine it with the active yeast.
2. Stir it carefully until the yeast is dissolved.
3. Then add brown sugar, vanilla extract, flour, and oatmeal flour.
4. Add salt and knead the soft but non-sticky dough.
5. Roll the dough and sprinkle it with the vanilla sugar.
6. The roll up the dough and cut it into rolls.
7. Sprinkle the vanilla rolls with the olive oil.
8. Preheat the air fryer to 365 F.
9. Put the vanilla rolls in the air fryer and cook them for 17 minutes.
10. Check the doneness of the rolls after 13 minutes of cooking.
11. When the vanilla rolls are cooked – chill them well.
12. Enjoy!

Nutrition: calories 143, fat 5.9, fiber 0.6, carbs 19.6, protein 2.1

Chocolate Vanilla Soufflé

Prep time: 15 minutes
Cooking time: 15 minutes
Servings: 2
Ingredients:

- 2 oz dark chocolate
- 3 tablespoon butter
- 2 eggs
- 1 oz flour
- 1 oz sugar
- ¼ teaspoon vanilla extract
- 2 teaspoon sugar, powdered

Directions:

1. Separate the egg yolks and egg whites.
2. Whisk the egg yolks with the sugar and vanilla extract.
3. Then melt the butter and dark chocolate.
4. Combine the butter and dark chocolate together.
5. Pour the mixture into the egg yolks and stir it.
6. Add flour and mix it until homogenous.
7. Then whisk the egg whites until the strong peaks.
8. Pour the chocolate mixture into the ramekins.
9. Then add the egg white mixture and stir it gently.
10. Preheat the air fryer to 330 F.
11. Put the ramekins in the air fryer basket and cook for 15 minutes.
12. When the soufflé is cooked let it chill briefly.
13. Sprinkle the surface of the soufflé with the powdered sugar.
14. Serve the soufflé only warm.
15. Enjoy!

Nutrition: calories 483, fat 30.2, fiber 1.3, carbs 44.7, protein 9.4

Almond Bars

Prep time: 15 minutes
Cooking time: 12 minutes
Servings: 2
Ingredients:

- 2 tablespoon sugar, powdered
- ¼ teaspoon baking powder
- 3 tablespoon butter, soft
- 3 tablespoon almond flour
- 2 oz almonds, crushed
- ½ teaspoon olive oil

Directions:

1. Combine together the soft butter, baking powder, powdered sugar, almond flour, and olive oil.
2. Knead the plastic dough.
3. Place the dough in the air fryer basket and sprinkle over with the crushed almonds.
4. Press the crushed almonds gently.
5. After this, preheat the air fryer to 360 F.
6. Cook the almond bar for 12 minutes.
7. After this, transfer the cooked almond bar into the serving plate.
8. Cut it into the servings.
9. Enjoy the almond bars immediately or keep them in the paper bags.

Nutrition: calories 435, fat 37.6, fiber 14.7, carbs 20.6, protein 8.4

Banana Pastries

Prep time: 15 minutes
Cooking time: 6 minutes
Servings: 2
Ingredients:

- 1 banana
- 2 filo sheets
- 1 teaspoon butter, melted
- ¼ teaspoon vanilla extract
- 1 tablespoon water
- ¼ teaspoon ground nutmeg

Directions:

1. Peel the banana and chop it.
2. Combine the chopped banana with the vanilla extract and ground nutmeg.
3. Then place together filo sheets and roll them.
4. Cut the filo sheets into 2 pieces.
5. Place the banana filling on the filo sheets and secure them to make the pastries.
6. Preheat the air fryer to 350 F.
7. Sprinkle the banana pastries with the water and put them in the air fryer basket.
8. Cook the pastries for 6 minutes.
9. When the dessert is cooked – serve it warm.
10. Enjoy!

Nutrition: calories 72, fat 2.2, fiber 1.6, carbs 13.7, protein 0.7

Banana Cinnamon Cake

Prep time: 10 minutes
Cooking time: 7 minutes
Servings: 2
Ingredients:

- 2 bananas
- 2 eggs
- 1 tablespoon oatmeal flour
- 1 teaspoon butter
- 2 teaspoon white sugar
- ¼ teaspoon ground cinnamon

Directions:

1. Peel the bananas and mash them with the help of the fork.
2. Beat the eggs in the mashed banana.
3. Add oatmeal flour, butter, white sugar, and ground cinnamon.
4. Mix the banana mixture with the help of the hand mixer.
5. After this, preheat the air fryer to 365 F.
6. Pour the mashed banana mixture into the air fryer basket and flatten it gently.
7. Cook the banana cake for 7 minutes.
8. The cooked cake should be very soft.
9. Chill it to the room temperature.
10. Enjoy!

Nutrition: calories 208, fat 6.8, fiber 3.5, carbs 32.8, protein 7.2

Caramel Popcorn

Prep time: 10 minutes
Cooking time: 15 minutes
Servings: 2
Ingredients:

- 1 cup corn kernels
- 1 teaspoon olive oil
- 2 tablespoon caramel

Directions:

1. Preheat the air fryer to 450 F.
2. Place the baking cage in the air fryer basket.
3. Put the corn kernels in the baking cage.
4. Cook the popcorn for 5 minutes.
5. After this, transfer the cooked popcorn to the bowl.
6. Sprinkle it with the caramel and shake well.
7. Spray the air fryer basket with the olive oil inside.
8. Put the caramel popcorn in the air fryer basket and cook it at 250 F for 10 minutes.
9. Shake the cooked caramel carefully and serve.
10. Enjoy!

Nutrition: calories 88, fat 3.3, fiber 2.1, carbs 14.7, protein 2.5

Chocolate Sugary Cupcakes

Prep time: 15 minutes
Cooking time: 10 minutes
Servings: 2
Ingredients:

- 2 tablespoon cocoa powder
- 1/3 teaspoon baking powder
- 1 teaspoon apple cider vinegar
- 2 teaspoon brown sugar
- 3 tablespoon butter
- 5 tablespoon flour
- 1 egg
- 2 tablespoon whipped cream
- ½ teaspoon lime zest

Directions:

1. Beta the egg in the mixing bowl and whisk it.
2. Add baking powder, apple cider vinegar, brown sugar, butter, cocoa powder, and flour.
3. Use the mixer to make the smooth cupcake dough.
4. Preheat the air fryer to 365 F.
5. Pour the cupcake dough into the cupcake molds.
6. Then place the cupcakes in the air fryer basket and cook for 10 minutes.
7. Cook for 2 extra minutes of desired.
8. Then remove the cupcakes from the air fryer and chill them well.
9. Sprinkle the cupcakes with the whipped cream.
10. Then sprinkle the lemon zest over the whipped cream.
11. Enjoy!

Nutrition: calories 324, fat 25, fiber 2.2, carbs 21.9, protein 6.3

Cinnamon Fried Bananas

Prep time: 10 minutes
Cooking time: 4 minutes
Servings: 2
Ingredients:

- 1 tablespoon maple syrup
- 2 teaspoon brown sugar
- 2 teaspoon butter
- 2 bananas
- 2 tablespoon oatmeal
- 1/3 teaspoon ground cinnamon
- 1 egg white, whisked

Directions:

1. Combine the whisked egg white with the brown sugar, ground cinnamon, and maple syrup.
2. Melt the butter and add it to the whisked egg white mixture.
3. Stir it carefully.
4. Peel the bananas and dip them in the egg white mixture.
5. Then sprinkle the bananas with the oatmeal generously.
6. Preheat the air fryer to 400 F.
7. Place the bananas in the air fryer basket and cook for 4 minutes.
8. Flip the bananas into another side after 2 minutes of cooking.
9. Serve the fried bananas only hot.
10. Enjoy!

Nutrition: calories 205, fat 4.6, fiber 3.8, carbs 40.5, protein 3.8

Marble Cocoa Cake

Prep time: 20 minutes
Cooking time: 16 minutes
Servings: 2
Ingredients:

- 1 pinch salt
- 2 teaspoon white sugar
- 1 tablespoon butter
- 1 egg
- 1 teaspoon cocoa powder
- ¼ teaspoon lemon juice
- 3 tablespoon flour

Directions:

1. Preheat the air fryer to 360 F.
2. Combine together a ½ tablespoon of butter and 1 teaspoon white sugar.
3. Mix the mixture well until you get the smooth paste.
4. Beat the egg in the separate bowl and whisk it.
5. Then pour ½ part of the whisked egg in the butter paste.
6. Add 1 tablespoon of flour, cocoa powder, and a pinch of salt.
7. Then whisk the mixture.
8. Combine together the remaining butter, sugar, flour, and whisked the egg.
9. Add lemon juice and stir it carefully.
10. Transfer the white butter mixture to the air fryer tray.
11. Then pour the chocolate mixture into the center of the white butter mixture.
12. Make the swirls with the help of the wooden stick.
13. Cook the marble cake for 16 minutes.
14. When the cake is cooked – chill it well.
15. Enjoy!

Nutrition: calories 111, fat 6, fiber 0.6, carbs 13.4, protein 1.4

Sugary French Palmier

Prep time: 10 minutes
Cooking time: 15 minutes
Servings: 2
Ingredients:

- 5 oz puff pastry
- 2 teaspoon brown sugar
- ½ teaspoon olive oil

Directions:

1. Roll the puff pastry.
2. Make the logs from the puff pastry and sprinkle them with the brown sugar.
3. Then roll the puff pastry logs from 2 sides until they meet each other.
4. Then sprinkle the air fryer basket with the olive oil.
5. Place the palmiers in the air fryer.
6. Cook the dessert for 15 minutes at 355 F.
7. When French palmiers are cooked – chill them well. Sprinkle the meal with the sugar again if desired.
8. Enjoy!

Nutrition: calories 412, fat 28.2, fiber 1.1, carbs 34.9, protein 5.2

Creamy Chakali

Prep time: 20 minutes
Cooking time: 5 minutes
Servings: 2
Ingredients:

- 3 tablespoon curd
- 3 tablespoon cornstarch
- 2 tablespoon cream
- 1 tablespoon flour
- ¼ teaspoon chili powder
- 1 teaspoon sugar
- 2 tablespoon olive oil

Directions:

1. Combine together the curd, cornstarch, cream, chili powder, sugar, and olive oil.
2. Knead the smooth and non-sticky dough.
3. Place it in the fridge for 10 minutes.
4. After this, place the dough in the pastry bag.
5. Make the medium cookies with the help of the round nozzle.
6. Place the chakali on the parchment.
7. Preheat the air fryer to 360 F.
8. Place the parchment with the chakali in the air fryer basket.
9. Cook the chakali for 5 minutes.
10. When the dessert is cooked – serve it immediately.
11. Enjoy!

Nutrition: calories 202, fat 15.6, fiber 0.2, carbs 14, protein 2.6

Vanilla Bread Pudding

Prep time: 15 minutes
Cooking time: 6 minutes
Servings: 2
Ingredients:

- 1 tablespoon cream
- 2 eggs
- 5 oz white bread
- 1 teaspoon vanilla extract
- 1 tablespoon butter
- 2 teaspoon brown sugar

Directions:

1. Beat the eggs in the bowl and whisk.
2. Chop the white bread into the tiny pieces and combine with the whisked egg.
3. Add cream, vanilla extract, butter, and brown sugar.
4. Mix the mixture carefully until homogenous.
5. Preheat the air fryer to 360 F.
6. Pour the bread mixture into the air fryer basket and cook for 6 minutes.
7. When the pudding is cooked – the surface should be light brown,
8. Transfer the cooked pudding to the serving plate.
9. Serve it only hot.
10. Enjoy!

Nutrition: calories 324, fat 12.8, fiber 1.7, carbs 39.6, protein 11.1

Oat Chocolate Chip Cookies

Prep time: 10 minutes
Cooking time: 7 minutes
Servings: 2
Ingredients:

- 1 tablespoon chocolate chips
- 3 tablespoon flour
- 3 tablespoon butter
- 1 tablespoon oatmeal
- 1 teaspoon lemon zest
- ¼ teaspoon vanilla sugar

Directions:

1. Melt the butter and combine it together with the chocolate chips and flour.
2. Add oatmeal, lemon zest, and vanilla sugar.
3. Mix the mixture carefully with the help of the spoon and then knead it with the help of the fingertips.
4. Make the medium balls from the dough and flatten them gently in the shape of the cookies.
5. Preheat the air fryer to 365 F.
6. Place the cookies in the air fryer basket and cook for 7 minutes. The time of cooking depends on the size of the cookies.
7. When the cookies are cooked – let them chill well and serve.
8. Enjoy!

Nutrition: calories 236, fat 19.1, fiber 0.8, carbs 14.5, protein 2.2

Banana Puff Rolls

Prep time: 15 minutes
Cooking time: 12 minutes
Servings: 2
Ingredients:

- 4 oz puff pastry
- 1 banana
- 2 ice cream balls
- 2 teaspoon butter
- 2 teaspoon water
- ½ tablespoon sugar

Directions:

1. Peel the banana and mash it with the help of the fork.
2. Roll the puff pastry and spread it with the mashed banana.
3. Melt the butter and combine it with the sugar.
4. Sprinkle the mashed banana with the melted butter mixture.
5. After this, roll the puff pastry and cut it into 2 servings.
6. Preheat the air fryer to 365 F.
7. Sprinkle the banana rolls with water and place it in the air fryer basket.
8. Cook the banana rolls for 12 minutes.
9. Placed the cooked banana rolls on the serving plates. The cooked meal should be a little bit crunchy.
10. Place the ice cream balls on the banana rolls and serve them.
11. Enjoy!

Nutrition: calories 547, fat 32.6, fiber 2.9, carbs 58.1, protein 7.1

Apple Pastry Dumplings

Prep time: 15 minutes
Cooking time: 20 minutes
Servings: 2
Ingredients:

- 1 green apple
- 1 egg yolk
- 2 teaspoon brown sugar
- 1 teaspoon butter
- ¼ teaspoon turmeric
- 6 oz puff pastry

Directions:

1. Chop the green apple into the small pieces.
2. Combine together the chopped apple, butter, brown sugar, and turmeric.
3. Shake the mixture well.
4. Roll the puff pastry with the help of the rolling pin and cut it into the squares.
5. After this, place the apple mixture in the center of every square and wrap them in the shape of the dumpling.
6. Whisk the egg yolk and brush the dumplings.
7. Preheat the air fryer to 357 F.
8. Place the dumplings in the air fryer and cook for 20 minutes.
9. Then serve the cooked apple dumpling immediately. The meal is tasty only when it is hot.
10. Enjoy!

Nutrition: calories 583, fat 6.8, fiber 4, carbs 57.2, protein 7.9

NY Cream Cheesecake

Prep time: 15 minutes
Cooking time: 37 minutes
Servings: 2
Ingredients:

- 2 eggs
- 7 oz cream cheese
- 2 tablespoon sugar, powdered
- ¼ teaspoon vanilla extract
- 4 tablespoon flour
- 2 tablespoon butter

Directions:

1. Beat the eggs in the bowl and whisk them together with the cream cheese and powdered sugar.
2. After this, combine together flour and 1 tablespoon of butter.
3. Knead the soft, non-sticky dough.
4. Place the dough in the air fryer cake tin and flatten it in the shape of the cheesecake crust.
5. Preheat the air fryer to 360 F and cook the crust for 12 minutes.
6. After this, remove the cheesecake crust from the air fryer and crumble it well.
7. Then combine the crumbled cheesecake crust with the remaining butter and make the homogenous mass.
8. Place the mass in the air fryer cake tin again.
9. Then flatten it well.
10. Pour the cream cheese mixture over the cheesecake crust and flatten it with the help of the plastic spatula.
11. Cook the cheesecake for 25 minutes at 360 F.
12. When the cheesecake is cooked chill it for at least 2 hours.
13. Enjoy!

Nutrition: calories 614, fat 50.6, fiber 0.4, carbs 27, protein 14.8

Cinnamon Churros

Prep time: 10 minutes
Cooking time: 6 minute
Servings: 2
Ingredients:

- ¼ cup water, hot
- 1 egg
- 1 pinch salt
- 1/3 cup flour
- 1 tablespoon butter
- 1 tablespoon brown sugar
- 1 teaspoon ground cinnamon

Directions:

1. Combine together flour, butter, salt, and hot water.
2. Mix the mixture until smooth.
3. Then beat the egg in the flour mixture and mix it with the help of the hand mixer.
4. Fill the piping bag with the dough.
5. Cover the air fryer basket with the parchment.
6. Make the small sticks (churros) from the dough.
7. Preheat the air fryer to 400 F and cook the meal for 6 minutes.
8. Meanwhile, combine together the brown sugar and ground cinnamon.
9. Toss the cooked churros to the sugar mixture and coat well.
10. Serve the dessert and enjoy!

Nutrition: calories 178, fat 8.2, fiber 1.2, carbs 21.4, protein 5

Banana Bread

Prep time: 15 minutes
Cooking time: 25 minutes
Servings: 2
Ingredients:

- 4 tablespoon flour
- 2 banana
- 1 egg
- 3 tablespoon cream
- ¼ teaspoon baking soda
- 2 teaspoon brown sugar

Directions:

1. Peel the bananas and mash them.
2. Combine together the mashed bananas and flour.
3. Beat the egg in the banana mixture.
4. Add cream, baking soda, and brown sugar.
5. Mix the mixture well.
6. Take the loaf mold and transfer the dough there.
7. Preheat the air fryer to 360 F.
8. Place the loaf mold in the air fryer and cook for 10 minutes.
9. After this, reduce the temperature to 350 F and cook the banana bread for 15 minutes more.
10. When the banana bread is cooked – discard it from the mold and chill it well.
11. Enjoy!

Nutrition: calories 216, fat 3.7, fiber 3.5, carbs 42.6, protein 5.8

Apple Pastry Roses

Prep time: 10 minutes
Cooking time: 7 minutes
Servings: 2
Ingredients:

- 1 apple
- 3 oz puff pastry
- 1 tablespoon white sugar
- 1 teaspoon butter

Directions:

1. Roll out the dough thinly.
2. Slice the apple thinly.
3. Then place the sliced apples over the dough.
4. Roll the dough into the medium roses.
5. Preheat the air fryer to 360 F.
6. Spread the air fryer basket with the butter and put the roses there.
7. Cook the apple roses for 7 minutes.
8. When the roses are cooked – chill them gently.
9. Enjoy!

Nutrition: calories 332, fat 18.3, fiber 3.3, carbs 40.6, protein 3.4

Creamy Caramel Muffins

Prep time: 10 minutes
Cooking time: 12 minutes
Servings: 2
Ingredients:

- 1 oz caramel
- 1 egg
- 4 oz sour cream
- 1/3 teaspoon baking powder
- 4 tablespoon flour
- 2 teaspoon white sugar
- 1 teaspoon butter

Directions:

1. Beat the egg in the mixing bowl and whisk it.
2. Add sour cream and baking powder.
3. After this, add flour, white sugar, and butter.
4. Use the mixer to make the smooth mass.
5. Then pour the dough into the muffin molds.
6. Fill the piping bag with the caramel.
7. Fill the muffin dough with the caramel.
8. Preheat the air fryer to 365 F.
9. Place the muffins in the air fryer basket and cook them for 12 minutes.
10. When the caramel muffins are cooked – chill them and discard from the muffin molds.
11. Serve the dessert!

Nutrition: calories 296, fat 17.3, fiber 0.4, carbs 29.8, protein 6.8

Milky Semolina Cake

Prep time: 15 minutes
Cooking time: 6 minutes
Servings: 2
Ingredients:

- 4 tablespoon semolina
- 8 tablespoon milk
- 1 tablespoon flour
- 2 tablespoon white sugar
- 1 teaspoon butter
- 1 egg yolk
- 1 teaspoon vanilla extract

Directions:

1. Combine together semolina and milk.
2. Whisk the egg yolk in the separate bowl.
3. Add flour and white sugar.
4. After this, combine together semolina mixture and egg yolk mixture.
5. Add butter and vanilla extract. Whisk it well.
6. Preheat the air fryer to 400 F.
7. Place the semolina mixture in the air fryer basket and cook it for 6 minutes.
8. When the cake is cooked – it will have golden brown surface.
9. Enjoy it warm!

Nutrition: calories 215, fat 5.7, fiber 0.9, carbs 33.8, protein 6.4

Plum Jam Tarts

Prep time: 20 minutes
Cooking time: 15 minutes
Servings: 2
Ingredients:

- ¼ teaspoon active yeast
- 1 pinch salt
- 2 teaspoon white sugar
- 2 tablespoon jam
- ¼ cup whey
- 6 tablespoon flour
- 1 teaspoon butter

Directions:

1. Preheat whey gently and add the active yeast.
2. Whisk the mixture until smooth.
3. Then add salt, white sugar, and flour.
4. Knead the smooth dough. Add more flour if desired.
5. Then roll out the dough.
6. Separate the dough into 2 parts.
7. Take 2 mini cake tins and place the dough there.
8. Leave the dough for 10 minutes to make it rise.
9. Spread the dough with the jam.
10. Place the butter over the jam.
11. Preheat the air fryer to 365 F.
12. Put the tarts in the air fryer basket.
13. Cook the tarts for 10 minutes.
14. Then reduce the temperature to 350 F and cook the tarts for 5 minutes more.
15. Chill the tarts till the room temperature.
16. Enjoy!

Nutrition: calories 207, fat 2.6, fiber 1, carbs 42.2, protein 3.8

Pumpkin Egg Mousse

Prep time: 10 minutes
Cooking time: 13 minutes
Servings: 2
Ingredients:

- 6 oz pumpkin puree
- 3 egg yolks
- 2 eggs, beaten
- 2 tablespoon brown sugar
- 1 tablespoon butter
- 1 teaspoon pumpkin pie spices

Directions:

1. Combine together egg yolks and eggs.
2. Mix them carefully with the help of the mixer.
3. Add brown sugar and pumpkin pie spices.
4. Then melt the butter and add it to the egg mixture.
5. Add pumpkin puree and stir it carefully with the help of the spatula.
6. Preheat the air fryer to 350 F.
7. Pour the pumpkin puree mixture into 2 ramekins.
8. Place the ramekins in the air fryer and cook for 13 minutes.
9. Whisk the mousse every 3 minutes during cooking.
10. When the mousse is cooked – chill it gently.
11. Serve it!

Nutrition: calories 261, fat 17.3, fiber 2.6, carbs 17.6, protein 10.6

Strawberry Cobbler

Prep time: 15 minutes
Cooking time: 10 minutes
Servings: 2
Ingredients:

- 2 tablespoon flour
- 1 teaspoon butter
- 1 teaspoon vanilla extract
- 1 egg
- 2 teaspoon white sugar
- 3 oz strawberries, chopped

Directions:

1. Combine together chopped strawberries and vanilla extract. Add sugar and stir the mixture.
2. Then combine together flour and butter.
3. Beat the egg in the flour mixture and mix it well.
4. Place the strawberry mixture into 2 ramekins.
5. Separate the dough into 2 parts.
6. Roll out the dough into the shape of the ramekins.
7. Then cover the strawberries with the dough and secure the edges.
8. Make the X cut in the center of the dough.
9. Cover the ramekins with the foil
10. Preheat the air fryer to 350 F.
11. Put the ramekins in the air fryer basket and cook the cobbler for 10 minutes.
12. The discard the foil and chill the meal.
13. Enjoy!

Nutrition: calories 111, fat 4.3, fiber 1.1, carbs 13.7, protein 3.9

Vanilla Plum Crumble

Prep time: 20 minutes
Cooking time: 22 minutes
Servings: 2
Ingredients:

- 4 plums, pitted
- 2 tablespoon butter
- 4 tablespoon flour
- ¼ teaspoon vanilla extract
- 2 tablespoon brown sugar
- 1 tablespoon sugar, powdered
- ¼ teaspoon ground nutmeg

Directions:

1. Chop the plums.
2. Melt the butter and combine it with flour and vanilla extract.
3. Mix the mixture until you get the soft dough.
4. Place the dough in the freezer for 15 minutes.
5. Meanwhile, combine together the chopped plums and brown sugar. Stir the mixture.
6. Remove the frozen dough from the freezer and grate it.
7. Then separate the dough into parts.
8. Sprinkle the air fryer cake tin with the first part of the dough.
9. Then spread the dough over the chopped plums.
10. Sprinkle the plum surface with the all remaining dough.
11. Preheat the air fryer to 360 F.
12. Cook the crumble for 22 minutes.
13. When the crumble is cooked – it should be a little bit crunchy.
14. Chill it to the room temperature.
15. Enjoy!

Nutrition: calories 278, fat 12.2, fiber 2.3, carbs 43, protein 2.8

Appendix:RecipesIndex

A

Almond Bars 122
Apple Pastries 120
Apple Pastry Dumplings 128
Apple Pastry Roses 130
Apricot Cinnamon Crumble 115
Asparagus & Parmesan 59
Avocado Cheddar Rolls 7
Avocado Eggs 28
Avocado Sushi 91

B

Bacon Eggs 98
Bacon Mozzarella 106
Bacon Zucchini Boats 12
Baked Cheddar Eggs 12
Banana Bread 130
Banana Cinnamon Cake 123
Banana Oatmeal Bites 111
Banana Pancakes 25
Banana Pastries 123
Banana Puff Rolls 128
Beef Burgers 101
Beef Zucchini Rings 43
Bell Pepper Slices 65
Breakfast Parmesan Sandwich 13
Broccoli Parmesan Casserole 6
Butter Chicken Drumsticks 39
Butternut Squash Puree 70
Buttery Potato Scramble 14

C

Cabbage Beef Rolls 45
Cabbage with Tomato 72
Cake with Vanilla Frosting 118
Caramel Popcorn 124
Carrot & Potato Balls 103
Carrot Chips 87
Carrot Lentil Burgers 59
Cashew Cookies 120
Catfish Nuggets 32
Catfish Sticks 84
Cayenne Lamb Steak 52
Cayenne Pepper Brussels Sprouts 64
Celery Chicken Wings 38
Celery Pork Balls 100
Chard with Cheddar 75
Cheddar Baked Paprika Toasts 13
Cheddar Bread Pizza 19
Cheddar Chicken Breast 50
Cheddar Crumpets 30
Cheddar Eggs Burrito 8
Cheddar Hash Browns 18
Cheddar Hot Dogs 95
Cheddar Mac'n'Cheese 68
Cheddar Portobello Mushrooms 63
Cheddar Potato Gratin 58
Cheddar Potato Halves 23
Cheddar Zucchini Frittata 21
Cheese Oatmeal Fritters 26
Cherry Crust Pie 112
Chicken Mini Pies 102
Chicken Mushroom Rolls 22
Chicken Oatmeal Schnitzel 35
Chicken Sausages 6
Chicken Strips 24
Chili Bacon Slices 90
Chili Pork Slices 47
Chili Squash Wedges 80
Chocolate Butter Balls 114
Chocolate Chip Muffins 116
Chocolate Sauce 119
Chocolate Sugary Cupcakes 124
Chocolate Vanilla Soufflé 122
Cilantro Eggplant Chips 102
Cinnamon Apple Rings 94
Cinnamon Churros 129
Cinnamon Dough Bites 93
Cinnamon Doughnuts 115
Cinnamon French Toast 16
Cinnamon Fried Bananas 125
Cocoa Brownies 117
Coconut Chili Beef Strips 55
Coriander Shrimp Cakes 96
Corn & Beans Fries 89
Corn Apple Tots 104
Corn Okra Bites 88
Corn on Cobs 60
Cottage Cheese Mushrooms 81
Cracker Cheesecake 110
Cream Cheese Baked Potato 64
Cream Cheese Cauliflower 78
Cream Cheese Spinach 66
Cream Cheesecake Soufflé 113
Cream Potato 70
Creamy Bacon Omelet 11
Creamy Broccoli Florets 69
Creamy Caramel Muffins 131
Creamy Cauliflower Head 63
Creamy Chakali 126
Creamy Chicken Liver 84
Creamy Chocolate Profiteroles 113
Creamy Cod Fillet 39
Creamy Coriander Tilapia 32
Creamy Leek 66
Creamy Red Potatoes 82
Creamy Salmon Pieces 106
Cremini Mushroom Satay 62
Crunchy Avocado Sticks 97
Crunchy Catfish 37
Curry Chicken Breast 40

D

Dijon Chicken 54
Dijon Turkey Legs 43
Dill Mashed Potato 69
Dill Radish Fries 101

E

Egg Ham Rolls 14

Egg Sandwich 27
Eggplant & Zucchini Mix 74
Eggplant Ratatouille 62
Eggs in Bacon Cups 27
English Eggs Bacon Breakfast 10

F

Feta Beet Cubes 73
Feta Cheese Potato Slices 79
Figs with Goat Cheese 99

G

Garlic Catfish 33
Garlic Ground Chicken 36
Garlic Pork Satay 50
Ginger Apple Chips 85
Ginger Apricot Tart 110
Ginger Paprika Shrimps 51

H

Honey Banana Chips 85
Honey Carrots with Greens 82
Honey Pork Meatballs 49
Honey Pumpkin Delights 111
Honey Pumpkin Mash 25
Hot Beet Chips 107

I

Italian Beer Cod 33

K

Kale Chips 96

L

Leek Parmesan Tarts 28

M

Maple Carrot Fries 86
Maple Turkey Breast 41
Marble Cocoa Cake 125
Marinated Eggplants with Sesame Seeds 67
Marshmallow & Butter Bananas 119
Mayo Cauliflower Florets 92
Mexican Parmesan Corn 77
Milky Cod 21
Milky Egg Custard 109
Milky Semolina Cake 131
Milky Vanilla Toasts 11
Mozzarella Pepperoni Patties 19
Mozzarella Radish Salad 61
Mozzarella Sausage Stromboli 17
Mushrooms & Cream 77

N

Nutmeg Apricot Muffins 118
Nutmeg Blueberry Crumble 112
NY Cream Cheesecake 129

O

Oat Chicken Sausages 56
Oat Chocolate Chip Cookies 127
Oats Carrot Cookies 7
Oats Cookies 114
Olive Oil Okra 76
Onion Chicken Skin 48
Onion Green Beans 61
Orange Beef Mignon 34
Oregano Garlic Heads 73
Oregano Onion Rings 90
Oregano Pork Loaf 48

P

Paprika Chicken Bites 99
Paprika Chicken Buns 29
Paprika Corn Beef 42
Paprika Hasselback Potatoes 67
Paprika Soufflé 20
Paprika Yellow Squash 80
Parmesan Chicken Sticks 103
Parmesan Chorizo Rolls 30
Parmesan Egg Clouds 105
Parmesan Peppers 44
Parmesan Spinach Quiche 26
Parmesan Sweet Potato Casserole 57
Parmesan Zucchini Chips 98
Pepper Corn Fritters 95
Pepper Green Tomatoes 91
Pickles in Paprika 97
Pineapple Chicken Breast 31
Plum Jam Tarts 132
Pork Bak 46
Pork Chops 37
Pork Ribs 55
Pork Strips 31
Puff Cauliflower Patties 81
Pumpkin Egg Mousse 132

R

Raisin Vanilla Muffins 116
Raisins Carrot Pie 109
Ribeye Beef Steak 36
Rosemary Beef Steak 38
Rosemary Lamb Shank 53
Rosemary Salmon Steak 41
Running Cheddar Eggs 22

S

Salty Garlic Pretzels 94
Salty Lemon Artichokes 58
Salty Pork Belly 35
Salty Potato Chips 88
Scrambled Eggs 9
Sesame Pork Cubes 105
Sesame Tofu Cubes 83
Smoked Cashews 92
Smoked Salmon Omelet 29
Spicy Zucchini Slices 57
Spinach Fritters 100
Squid Rings 87
Strawberry Cobbler 133
Strawberry Oatmeal 18
Stuffed Calamari 42
Sugary Apple Fritters 89
Sugary Carrot Strips 60
Sugary French Palmier 126
Sugary Oatmeal Muffins 15
Sugary Pumpkin Wedges 65
Sweet Onion Rings 76
Sweet Potato Cubes 75
Sweet Potato Fries 86
Sweet Pumpkin Loaf 108

T

Tabasco Chicken Meatballs 20
Tahini Eggplants 78
Tender Beef Burgers 49
Thyme Fennel 79
Thyme Lamb Ribs 40
Thyme Salty Tomatoes 83
Toasted Salty Walnuts 93
Tofu Potato Scramble 15
Tomato Beef 51
Tomato Nutmeg Zucchini 71
Turkey Bread Reuben 9
Turmeric Carrot Balls 104
Turmeric Chicken Necks 53
Turmeric Potato 10
Turmeric Potato Pancakes 8
Turmeric Snapper 34

V

Vanilla Bread Pudding 127
Vanilla Bread Pudding 17
Vanilla Oat Rolls 121
Vanilla Plum Crumble 133

W

Walnut Baked Apples 117
White Oregano Cabbage 68
Wrapped Bacon Eggs 24

Y

Yogurt Chicken Kebab 54

CPSIA information can be obtained
at www.ICGtesting.com
Printed in the USA
LVHW061923131020
668706LV00022B/157

9 781649 845818